The Comic Vision
and the Christian Faith

For the name of these gods there is both a serious and a humorous explanation. The serious explanation is not to be had from me, but there is no hindrance to my offering the humorous one, for the gods too are fond of a joke.

—Socrates in Cratylus

The Comic Vision and the Christian Faith

A Celebration of Life and Laughter

Conrad Hyers

The Pilgrim Press
New York

Library of Congress Cataloging in Publication Data

Hyers, M. Conrad.
  The comic vision and the Christian faith.

  Bibliography: p. 192
  1. Christianity and humor. 2. Comedy. I. Title.
  BR115.H84H9   248.4   81-5221
  ISBN 0-8298-0440-4 (pbk.)   AACR2

Biblical quotations are from the *Revised Standard Version of the Bible*, copyright 1946, 1952 and © 1971 by the Division of Christian Education, National Council of Churches, and are used by permission. The excerpt from "Little Gidding" at note 18 in chapter 6 is from *Four Quartets* by T. S. Eliot. Copyright 1943 by T.S. Eliot; renewed 1971 by Esme Valerie Eliot. Reprinted by permission of Harcourt Brace Jovanovich, Inc. and Faber and Faber Ltd. (London). The lines from "Chaplinesque" at note 6 in chapter 7 are from *The Complete Poems and Selected Letters and Prose of Hart Crane*, edited by Brom Weber, and are reprinted by permission of Liveright Publishing Corporation. Copyright 1933, © 1958, 1966 by Liveright Publishing Corporation. The three lines of haiku at note 8 in chapter 7 are from "The Flower Wreath," *An Introduction to Haiku*, translated by Harold G. Henderson. Reprinted by permission of Doubleday & Company, Inc. Some of the material in this book is based on essays by Conrad Hyers in *The Christian Century*: "The Recovery of Simplicity" (August 7-14, 1974) and "The Nativity as Divine Comedy" (December 11, 1974), copyright 1974 Christian Century Foundation, and "Farewell to the Clown: A Tribute to Charlie" (February 22, 1978), copyright 1978 Christian Century Foundation. Used by permission.

The Pilgrim Press, 132 West 31 Street, New York, New York 10001

Contents

In appreciation for
the inspired folly of three friends:

Father Nick Weber, S.J.,
Royal Lichtenstein Quarter-Ring Sidewalk Circus

Father John Naus, S.J.,
Tumbleweed the Clown

Ken Feit, Fool

Acknowledgments

Grateful appreciation is due the National Endowment for the Humanities for providing a research fellowship to explore the symbolic significance of the comic tradition and its relationship to religious themes and values. I also wish to recognize the many students of the past ten years at Beloit College and at Gustavus Adolphus College, as well as in summer conferences and Elderhostel programs, who have mused with me, and been amused and bemused, over the many forms and faces of the comic muse.

I am indebted to many sources of inspiration and assistance: to Chad Walsh, who encouraged me in the fledgling stages of my study; to Nathan Scott, Jr.—who has written the finest single essay on the subject—for the good influences of his insight and example; to Mircea Eliade, who first engaged me in the analysis of myth, ritual, and symbol; to John Hick, my former mentor, who led me into issues that have now borne this unusual fruit; to Bardwell Smith, who has provided needed moral support and his own kindly sense of humor; to William Dean, who has given me the benefit of penetrating criticism; to Luke Reinsma, who has offered helpful editorial suggestions; and, not least, to my grandmother, whose rollicking laugh and bubbling disposition—into her eighty-seventh year—have stayed with me.

I must also acknowledge a special indebtedness to the artistry of Charles Chaplin, whose films I had not seen until a few years ago but from whom I have learned more than from any other source. For several decades Charlie was one of the most widely known and beloved figures in the world, not only because he was a master clown communicating through the universal language of pantomime, but also because he grappled comically with universal human problems. With soulful eyes in a pallid face, his shabby but once elegant clothes, his jaunty penguin gait, his dusty dignity, Charlie touched the heart of the human condition in a way that was as profoundly religious as it was profoundly humorous. Though he denied having much knowledge of religious doctrines and affairs—beyond the stories and impressions he picked up in early youth at religious meetings in the slums of London—he nevertheless displayed a deeply human sensitivity that offered much more than a slapstick performance and a laughter of the moment.

At the end of his last "silent" film, *The Great Dictator* (1940), Chaplin broke the silence he had maintained for twenty-five years—and well into the era of the "talkies"—as if compelled to deliver the message of his clowning in unmistakable terms. As a refugee Jewish barber fleeing toward the Austrian border, Charlie has been mistaken for the German dictator and is chauffered to a waiting crowd at a nearby Nazi rally. Hesitantly and haltingly he begins:

I'm sorry, but I don't want to be an emperor. That's not my business. I don't want to rule or conquer anyone. I should like to help everyone—if possible—Jew, Gentile; black men, white.

We all want to help one another. Human beings are like that. We want to live by each other's happiness—not by each other's misery. We don't want to hate and despise one another. In this world there is room for everyone. And the good earth is rich and can provide for everyone.[1]

That, essentially, is the clown's credo. It is a faith and a confession that is at the heart of both the comic vision and the Christian faith. And we are indebted to a great comic artist for putting it so simply and succinctly, as in his pantomime he put it so unforgettably.

The Gift of Laughter

A posthumously published letter to W. C. Fields from a niece in Ireland informed him in 1940:

Your cousin Hughie Dougherty was hung in Londonderry last Friday for killing a policeman. May God rest his soul and may God's curse be on Jimmy Rodger, the informer. May his soul burn in hell. God forgive me. . . .

Times are not as bad as they might be. The herring is back . . . and the price of fish is good, thanks be to God. The Black and Tans are terrible. They go through the country in their lorries and shoot the poor people down in the fields where they are working. God's curse on them.

Your Uncle Danny took a shot at one of them yesterday from the hedge, but he had too much to drink and missed them. God's curse on drink. . . .

P.S. Things might be worse than they are. Every police barrack and every Protestant church in the country has been burned down. Thanks be to God.[1]

The letter was not intended to be humorous, and the religious conflicts to which it refers are certainly tragic. But the inconsistencies displayed are nevertheless humorous, especially because the writer is so oblivious to them. A previous letter had ended even more incongruously: "Your Aunt Maggie from Ireland, who has informed me

The W. C. Fields material above is from the book *W.C. Fields by Himself* by W. C. Fields. © 1973 by W. C. Fields Productions, Inc. Published by Prentice-Hall, Inc., Englewood Cliffs, NJ 07632. Used by permission.

that more Protestant churches have been burned to the ground, sends her love.''

The comic tradition deals, among other things, with such incongruities, exposing them, softening them, and hopefully in some measure preventing them. Like anything else of value, however, the comic spirit and perspective must be cultivated. Laughter and humor may be natural to the species, but they do not automatically reach full flower, or grace the whole of life. In some contexts they may even be shunned or suppressed as inappropriate, and left quite undeveloped.

Nearly seventy years ago William Austin Smith made bold to suggest:

Every Divinity School might well have in its senior year, along with courses in systematic divinity and homiletics, a course in the great masters of comedy; and, to arouse our sluggish wits and keep us on our guard, it might not be amiss to carve upon our pulpits, side by side with the lean Gothic saints, the figure of Aristophanes or Molière with warning finger.[2]

The suggestion has not been diligently pursued in our seminaries or other institutions of higher learning. The prevailing attitude, if anything, has inclined in the opposite direction. And the calumny and vehemence that often characterize religious conflicts are continuing testimony to the failure to understand the *religious* importance—indeed, necessity—of the comic vision.

More revealing of traditional religious understandings is the eighteenth-century treatise by Richard Blackmore ironically titled *Satyr Against Wit*. Sir Richard saw unbridled wit and humor as the enemy of true religion, stalwart virtue, and right reason—a form of insanity and a seducer of young people. Later in the preface to his *Creation* he saw a definite link between witticism and atheism. And extending his argument further in a subsequent essay, he concluded that wit

has no place in history, philology, philosophy, or in the greater lyric or epic poems. . . . Lofty and illustrious subjects, such as the foundation, rise and revolution of kingdoms, commotions of state, battles, triumphs, solemn embassies, and various other important actions of princes and heroes, are exalted above the sphere of wit and humor.

It is an ancient and venerable viewpoint with respect to the more serious subjects that affect and concern us deeply. The similar warning of the German philosopher George Friedrich Meier is representative of the misgivings of more than German philosophers:

We are never to jest on or with things which, on account of their importance or weight, claim our utmost seriousness. There are things . . . so great and important in themselves, as never to be thought of and mentioned but with much sedateness and solemnity. Laughter on such occasions is criminal and indecent. . . . For instance, all jests on religion, philosophy, and the like important subjects.[3]

Yet our failure to entertain the jester "on such occasions" may be one of the primary sources of the "criminal and indecent" behavior that our "utmost seriousness" so often produces.

When Marcel Marceau divides his pantomime performances into a serious, dramatic program followed by a lighthearted comic one, we are moved in the right direction. The comic side of human nature and perception is given expression and celebration. Yet the relationship between the dramatic Marceau and the comic Marceau remains as unclear on stage as it is in human life generally. What does the latter have to say to or do with the former? What is added to the dramatic Marceau by the comic Marceau? Or are we simply to be left in this schizoid condition?

The situation is hardly improved by the fact that, though our educational systems sponsor innumerable courses in the appreciation of art, music, and literature, as well as gardening, cooking, and tennis, little is offered in the way of *comic* appreciation. This remarkable side of our existence as human beings, which actually tempers and qualifies everything else, is left adrift as a light distraction from more important concerns, a playful interlude whose justification is that it may help us let off a little steam now and then or provide a cheap vacation of the mind from which we will return to work more industriously and fight unquestioningly. To the most sober-minded, humor may even be seen as—in Chad Walsh's phrase—a kind of "wart on the human soul." Yet the ability to see the humor in things, or to create comic tales and rituals, is among the most profound and imaginative of human achievements. The comic sense is an important part of what it means to be human and humane. Without it we return to brutishness, and the Philistines are upon us.

There are, of course, those ultraserious types who claim not to be opposed to laughter as such but to consider it largely inappropriate—considering, that is, the current state of the union and the universe: This is not the time and place for laughter, only for diligence and vigilance. Playfulness of spirit is a frivolous and irresponsible luxury. There are letters to be written to congressional representatives, picket signs to be carried, committees to be organized, politicians to be badgered, votes to be garnered, opponents to be debated, corporations and administrations to be hounded, enemies to be defeated. There is little room for parades and balloons and anecdotes and idle chatter. With steeled jaw and knitted brow, looking neither to the right nor to the left, such humorless crusaders are unwilling and perhaps no longer able to laugh, as long as "the cause" has not been victorious, injustice prevails, poverty and pollution persist, warfare continues, textbooks are inaccurate, magazines are sexist—in short, as long as there is evil and suffering in the world—which is to say that they are not likely to be free to laugh in the near future.

To all such one must say: Blessed are they that can laugh outside the gates of Paradise and the New Jerusalem, and who there can give and receive the gift of laughter. Blessed are they who are not determined to wait until lions lie down with lambs, and who can pray, "O God, though I do not live in the Garden of Eden I am nevertheless still glad to be here."

The Breath of Life and Laughter

One of the reasons for a low view of the comic among us is that the Western tradition has no clear religious basis for laughter and humor. Neither of the biblical creation accounts, so influential in shaping Western culture, specifically mentions the creation of laughter and a sense of humor or indicates their place and function in human life. The Yahwist account of Genesis 2 does contain the potential for a comic understanding in the imagery of being created out of the dust of the earth, and of a divine potter making a clay figurine into which is breathed the breath of life, but it remains undeveloped.

In the mythologies of the world, human beings are created out of quite an array of things, for example, clots of blood, pieces of skin, minerals, eggs, stones. The biblical picture represents one of the more humble types, though perhaps not quite so humble as a myth from the aborigines of South Australia in which humans were created from excrement. The excrement was then molded into human form and tickled, thus causing the image to laugh and come alive.[4] Still, Adam, taken from the ground (*adamah*), is an earthy fellow; and Eve, taken from his side, has an equally unpretentious origin.

In the Yahwist narrative, Adam comes closest to a manifestation of laughter in his awakening to discover Eve at his side with a surprised delight in the creation of a companion. The logic of the story, in fact, suggests a kind of creation comedy, if one were otherwise disposed to view it in that light. Though Adam was placed in a garden paradise, with all his needs provided, the implication is that it was not a paradise for him because he was lonely. So, as if a divine experiment were set in motion to resolve the difficulty, God created animals. But despite all the jokes from sheep-herding societies to our own about people preferring faithful dogs to nagging spouses, Adam was still lonely. So God caused Adam to fall into a deep sleep, and when Adam woke up he found a woman at his side, taken from his rib. Adam rejoiced, "At last, bone of my bone and flesh of my flesh," or, as *The Living Bible* translates the enthusiasm, Adam on seeing Eve exclaimed, "This is it!" Male and female (*ish* and *ishshah*): the original unity and the original incongruity, and in both respects among the original sources of laughter.

While there is here no specific reference to laughter, it might be imagined as present in several forms, given the circumstances: the laughter of pleasant surprise; the laughter of joy and delight; the laughter of discovery and recognition; the laughter over a tension released and a problem resolved; the laughter of incongruity in Adam's suddenly seeing a reflection of himself in feminine form; the laughter of incredulity; the laughter of amazement and wonder; perhaps a laughter over the happy absurdity of sexual differentiation and sexual identity; and thus a laughter in the context of a newfound tension-in-unity, the relationship of male and female, which has certainly spawned its share of jokes and rib-tickling laughter ever since.

All this is conceivable. Mark Twain, in fact, made a convincing little comedy out of it, *Eve's Diary*. Still, none of these nuances is directly mentioned as such. And when subsequently read and interpreted by a sober piety, and mixed in with great haste for getting on to the subject of sin and guilt, any potential movement in this direction is lost from the beginning. We are left with not even a preliminary smile.

There *is* a myth, however, closely paralleling the biblical account, in which laughter is singled out as belonging to the culmination of human creation. Although unrelated, it provides clues as to how the biblical text might be imaginatively reconstructed. This, in summary form, is the myth as told among the Jicarilla Apache:

When Hactcin had created all the animals he stood back and looked at them. And he began to laugh at the sight of so many different kinds of creatures, with their different appearances and habits—which is why, it is said, people today laugh at the behavior of animals.

After the animals had been assigned their places and instructed in their ways, they held a council, and came to Hactcin and said, "We need a companion. You are not going to be with us all the time. We need someone like you to stay with us." So the animals gathered an assortment of objects and set them before Hactcin: pollen, iron ore, algae, red ochre, white clay, and various gems. Hactcin took the pollen and traced an outline of a figure on the ground, like himself. And inside the outline he placed the various objects, which became bones and flesh, skin, hair, and eyes.

Then the figure came to life. It was a man, lying face downward. The man began to move, and Hactcin told him to sit up. Then he picked the man upright and said to him four times, "Speak." And the man began to speak. Then he said to him, "Shout." And the man gave a big yell. Then Hactcin thought a while and said, "Laugh." And the man laughed. The dog was glad when he saw the man laugh. He jumped up on him, wagging his tail, and ran back and forth happily. Then Hactcin taught the man to walk and run. And when the birds saw what Hactcin had made, they sang and chirped as though it were early morning.

But the animals thought it was not good that man should be by himself. So they went to Hactcin and told him that the man too should have a companion. Hactcin agreed, and asked them to bring him some lice. He took the lice and put them on the man's head, causing him to itch and scratch. The scratching made him sleepy. And when he fell asleep, he dreamed that a creature like, yet unlike, him was sitting at his side. When he awoke the dream had come true. A young woman was sitting there. The man spoke to her, and to his astonishment she answered him. Then he began to laugh, and the woman laughed too. Together they laughed and laughed.[5]

It is unfortunate that neither of the creation stories in the Western biblical tradition gives such a fundamental and prominent place to the creation of laughter and a sense of humor. This not only leaves the matter of their function and importance in some doubt, it also opens the way for the suggestion that laughter and humor are of little critical significance or that they are not of the "order of creation." And if they are not of the order of creation, they are certainly not of the "order of redemption," and therefore are the creation of an evil spirit, or the consequence of human sin.

Though these are arguments from silence, they nevertheless represent some of the lines along which laughter and humor have been understood. The theme of divine laughter, which in the Apache myth is an enjoyment of the comical diversity of animal types, has easily been reduced to a taunting of the enemies of God (and Israel), as in Psalm 2: "He who sits in the heavens laughs; the Lord has them in derision." And human laughter, which in the Apache myth becomes one of the highest and most distinctive human characteristics, has easily been dismissed as detrimental to a holy seriousness, as in Robert Barclay's *Apology for the True Christian Divinity* (1676): "It is not lawful to use games, sports, plays, nor among other things comedies among Christians, under the notion of recreations, since they do not agree with Christian silence, gravity and sobriety; for laughing, sporting, gaming, mocking, jesting, vain talking, etc., is not Christian liberty, nor harmless mirth."[6] Much earlier (A.D. 390), Chrysostom had preached the same: "This world is not a theatre, in which we can laugh; and we are not assembled together in order to burst into peals of laughter, but to weep for our sins. . . . It is not God who gives us the chance to play, but the devil."[7]

It is no surprise to find that theologians and moralists, who have had much to say about seriousness and sobriety, have had little good to say about nonsense and laughter; there are many fine words about the responsibility to work, few about the "responsibility" to play. Still it is really as much in play as in work, in laughter as well as seriousness, and especially in the playfulness of humor, that humanity is differentiated from the rest of the animal kingdom. Christian theologians have expended copious efforts on the subject of the "image of God" in humanity. Yet for all these laborious and occasionally acrimonious deliberations, precious little has been said about laughter and humor as aspects of the *imago dei*, let alone as a dimension of the religious situation before the divine. The impression is given that laughter is the creation of the devil or a fumbling demiurge, or that it is a pale substitute left to Adam and Eve after their expulsion from the more holy joys of paradise. The ancient Greek peripatetics were closer to the true state of affairs when they characterized human beings as the "laughing animals" (*zoion gelastikon*) and saw in the comic sense one of the distinctive badges of humanity (*homo ridens*).

Perhaps a part of the historical inclination of Judaism, Christianity, and Islam (sharing as they do in the same creation mythology) toward dogmatism, intolerance, and even "holy war" has something to do with the lack of a specific grounding of laughter and humor in the divine nature, human nature, and human relationships. At the least, what is not stressed is not likely to be encouraged or cultivated. And it may expressly be *discouraged*.

Certainly the ultraserious image of Jesus which has prevailed through much of the history of the church would not so easily have suggested or perpetuated itself if laughter and humor had more obvious biblical footing. The image is hardly correct, as Elton Trueblood's *The Humor of Christ* demonstrates.[8] It was actually John the Baptist who was the "straight man" in the Gospels, coming "neither eating nor drinking" and "crying in the wilderness." Jesus, by contrast, began his ministry by turning water into wine at the marriage festivities in Cana and was accused of being "a glutton and a drunkard" and associating with "publicans and sinners." Though this image is no more correct than the superserious image, it reveals a side of Jesus which the pious imagination has tended to ignore or deny. The absence of any parenthetical notations in the Gospel records as to when Jesus may have smiled or laughed, and in what contexts, has always left the issue open for a one-sided interpretation to fill in the blank. Thus the medieval *Cursor Mundi* concludes: "That thrice he wept we find enough, but never where he laughed." Yet what does the full humanity of Jesus mean if it does not include the freedom of laughter and humor?

The problem is not unique to Christianity. Buddhist scholastics—not unlike Christian scholastics—had heated debates on the question whether the Buddha ever laughed, for laughter seemed inconsistent with the inner harmony and serenity that the Buddha was believed to have achieved, or the resolute discipline necessary to achieve it. Certain passages of scripture, however, seemed clearly to indicate that on such and such an occasion the Buddha *had* laughed. A solution to the apparent dilemma was found in a theatrical manual of the fourth century A.D.—even though Buddhist monks were not permitted to attend theatrical performances. The Indian dramatist Bharata had conveniently distinguished between six classes of laughter, as these were to be displayed on the stage, depending upon the caste and type of individual being portrayed. The most refined individuals were to be represented in the most restrained manner: *sita*, a faint smile, or *hasita*, a smile that barely revealed the tips of the teeth. The more average, or middle-caste, person was to be represented by moderate expression: *vihasita*, a broad smile accompanied by a modicum of laughter, and *upahasita*, a broader smile with louder laughter. It was only in representing the uncouth individual and the lowest caste that the actor was to engage in unrestrained laughter: *apahasita*, a laughter that brings tears, and *athasita*, a backslapping doubling over in raucous guffawing.[9]

Given this dramatic classification, the religious interpretation easily followed suit. The first two forms of "laughter" approach the spiritual and the sublime. The last two descend into the crassness and vulgarity of the sensual, lowering and degrading the spirit. And, as might be expected, the Buddha was supposed to have indulged only in *sita*, the most subtle and serene form of laughter. It is almost as if to say that the Buddha was only "guilty" of the most minimal and barely perceptible smile.

The Buddhist restrictions on laughter are reminiscent of reports made by certain anthropologists of missionary successes along these lines in Africa. Before the missionaries came the natives were noted for their hearty, full-bodied laughter. But unrestrained laughter seemed "pagan" to the missionaries. After their reeducation in Christian ways, the natives developed a nervous, suppressed, embarrassed laughter known as the "mission giggle."

Yet if one reinverts scholastic schemas, the unrestrained laughter of the whole person becomes the *highest* level of laughter and expresses the fullest measure of human freedom. The belly laugh is not the dark descent of spirit into flesh, or of sacred into profane, but the free and unitary expression of one's total being. The repression of laughter, and of the comic spirit, is not salvation but bondage. And its historical consequences are not liberation but inquisition and oppression.

The Priesthood of Comedy

Medieval physiology determined that the seat of laughter was the spleen.[10] This not very intellectually or spiritually promising location may have derived from the abdominal associations of laughter, which seemed to well up and explode in the larynx from some dark, abysmal region. Laughter belonged to the lower levels of our beings, in association with the stomach, intestines, sex organs, and bladder. By identifying laughter with the spleen rather than the brain or heart, let alone spirit, the rational and religious values of a comic sensitivity were easily dismissed.

One of the striking features of the comic tradition, however, is that nothing stands entirely outside its purview. It is not merely tangential to life, or something from the cellar of life, but all-encompassing. No circumstance is so lowly or inconsequential that comedy will not grant it an audience. Nor is any authority so high, or any subject so dear, that comedy has failed to approach it in more than fear and trembling.

So inclusive is the comic vision that one may see in it a kind of mythology, with a symbol system of its own, which it brings to all aspects of our lives, including those persons and things of utmost importance. The great array of comic figures—tricksters, clowns, fools, jesters, humorists, comedians, and the like—are the officiants of this tradition: its heroes and sages, its "prophets, priests, and kings." They are the caretakers of its myths and symbols, exemplars of its vision, defenders of its faith, and celebrants of its rituals.

Comic performances are often credited with dealing essentially in trifles and irrelevancies. Close examination, however, shows that this is far from the case. And even when it *is* the case, "trifling irrelevancy" is not the whole point. Nearly all, if not all, the major issues with which human beings have concerned themselves are dealt with in some manner in the comic tradition. All the central religious categories, for example, are there: creation, celebration, mystery, wonder, finitude, pride, humility, justice, iconoclasm, salvation, hope, eschatology, and so on. The "heroes" and "high priests" of comedy also function in ways that are analogous to their dramatic and religious counterparts, and stand in special relationship to them.

True, we do not customarily associate comic figures with religious ones. And comic figures seem more adept at profaning holy things than supporting them. Yet their odd antics and odd words and odd attire carry a profound symbolism, with a consistent mythic structure and ritual movement. So much is this the case that one may speak not only of the comedy of religion but also of the religion of comedy.

The essays here presented are aimed at a comic appreciation of these comic figures and their meaning, that is, at the enrichment of life through the art of comedy. The goal is not purely an academic one. And the text has not been compacted—in the words of the subtitle to William Derham's seventeenth-century treatise on *Physico-Theology*—"with large notes and many curious observations." To offer an extended scholarly disquisition on the comic would be to pile incongruity upon incongruity and run the risk of choking the comic spirit rather than promoting it. There is an inherent falsification of the subject matter in any attempt to write completely without humor about human beings and their concerns—above all when the subject matter is the comic itself. The style, accordingly, is more poetic than didactic, and the tone seeks to preserve some of the lightheartedness that is the object of inquiry.

"Meditations," would perhaps be an accurate description of the essays, if that term may be taken in the philosophical rather than devotional or sermonic sense. A meditation is a form of intellectual and emotional savoring that enables one to both enjoy and digest the meal, not just analyze the recipe ad nauseum. The book, however, is not as such a comic production, any more than a treatise on cooking is necessarily a culinary delight.

Books have been written on one or another aspect of the comic tradition from a variety of perspectives: literature, drama, sociology, psychology, anthropology, philosophy, classics, theology, and even biology. The following essays take a fresh look from the standpoint of comparative mythology and the history of religions. While drawing upon other fields and studies, the orientation is that of the interpretation of myth, ritual, and symbol. And the focus is on the *religious significance* of the various comic forms.

Questions of the *function* of the comic—psychological, sociological, political, biological—will be touched upon, as well as questions of comic structure. But the larger questions have to do with the *meaning* of this side of existence. What are the implications of the comic perspective for those peculiarly human issues of sacred and profane, "truth, beauty, and goodness," "nature, man, and God"? What does this angle of vision reveal about human existence, or existence as such?

Functionalism and structuralism are not enough. And restricting the discussion to these levels, however sympathetic the treatment, would be reminiscent of that encomium of laughter given by the nineteenth-century Prussian professor Gottlieb Hufeland:

Laughter is one of the most important helps to digestion with which we are acquainted; and the custom in vogue among our ancestors, of exciting it by jesters and buffoons, was founded on true medical principles. Cheerful and joyous companions are invaluable at meals. Obtain such, if possible, for the nourishment received amid mirth and jollity is productive of light and healthy blood.

A glut of comic fare is certainly available for the production of light and healthy blood in contemporary television and radio programming, cinema, theater, magazines, advertisements, commercials, and books of cartoons and jokes. Yet without a profound understanding of this side of our existence and its potential implications, we may not be carried very far by a mass production of comic forms. Getting the point of a joke is not the same as getting the point of joking.

What is needed, furthermore, is not a running commentary on certain popular samples of the day, but a much broader context that will enable us to see better who and where we are. The examples used in the following essays, therefore, cover the whole span of the comic tradition and its principal types, from tribal ritual to circus clowning, from Greek comedy to modern cinema, from the ancient trickster to the animated cartoon. The result is not an extended footnote to some fashion of the decade, but a celebration of a spirit and perspective that belong to the archetypal "eternity" of the race and that need to be rehearsed now and then lest we, as Sören Kierkegaard put it, "succeed in making an advance upon Socrates, without first having understood what Socrates himself understood."

Among the Kurnai of Australia is a myth in which the waters of the earth had been swallowed by a great frog named Dak. The thirsty animals tried to get Dak to cough up the waters, but their efforts were in vain. Dak greedily remained stubborn and adamant. Finally the snake began twisting and rolling about in a most comical fashion. Dak tried to maintain a straight face with resolute determination, but could not—whereupon Dak burst out laughing, and the waters streamed forth to soak the parched earth.[11] The Kurnai myth-makers were primarily interested in the water, but for anyone interested in the laughter as well, the imagery of the tale may be given another meaning: Laughter bursts out of the small world of our seriousness and greed and self-importance and allows the water of life to flow freely to all, relieving the dryness and barrenness of our parched spirits.

Chapter 1

A Voice Laughing in the Wilderness

That's the first thing that got me about this place, there wasn't anybody laughing. I haven't heard a real laugh since I came through that door. . . . Man, when you lose your laugh you lose your footing.
—Randall Patrick McMurphy in
One Flew over the Cuckoo's Nest[1]

The last person known to have laughed in the United States was Robert Ketchum in 1984 in Salem, Massachusetts. As a result of his lack of seriousness and his bold impropriety, he was publicly burned at the stake by the local authorities. All three television networks covered the event.

Such was the tongue-in-cheek Orwellian prophecy offered by Art Buchwald in the midst of the radicalism of establishment and antiestablishment confrontations in the decade of the 1960s. It was the humorist's warning. Unqualified seriousness is dehumanizing and dangerous. It is the crucifier of freedom and the human spirit. And this is true whether one has in mind radicals of some right or left, or the more or less acquiescent middle. Humanity cannot live by seriousness alone.

In some respects it might seem that the prophecy had already come true, if the enormities perpetrated in the twentieth century in the name of racial purity or national superiority, ideological truth or political necessity, are any index. And perhaps in a much longer view of history one would come to conclude that the problem is coterminous with the species. The prophecy was fulfilled in the beginning; The fall of Adam was a fall into seriousness. And we have taken ourselves, our circumstances, our achievements, and our beliefs quite seriously ever since.

Yet there is a contemporary urgency about the question of laughter, if for no other reason than that we, more than any previous generation, have eaten so much more of the fruit of Adam's tree. An unparalleled knowledge and power is available to us for dehumanizing and destroying, as well as benefiting, one another. Fanaticism, terrorism, and oppression are more potent forces than ever before, given the latest technological capabilities. It is more imperative than ever that we understand the peculiarly human gift of laughter, and the comic sensibility that it expresses, if the prospect of greater tyrannies and holocausts is to be averted.

As Konrad Lorenz suggests in concluding his important study *On Aggression*, the survival of civilization depends to a significant degree upon our capacity for humor. People who laugh together are less inclined to kill one another. Humor, among other things, is a valuable mechanism for ritualizing aggressive impulses in substitution for the more violent and destructive means available to us. And it can provide a larger perspective in relation to ourselves, our scientific accomplishments and ideological persuasions.[2] Sanity and humanity, as McMurphy, the affable rogue in Ken Kesey's *One Flew over the Cuckoo's Nest*, understood the moment he entered the insane asylum, are impossible apart from humor.

The Seriousness of Humor

In one of Mark Twain's tall tales he tells how exercised he had become about the considerable amount of discord among God's creatures and how he had decided to take the matter in hand.

So I built a cage, and in it I put a dog and a cat. And after a little training I got the dog and the cat to the point where they lived peaceably together. Then I introduced a pig, a goat, a kangaroo, some birds and a monkey. And after a few adjustments, they learned to live in harmony. So encouraged was I by such successes that I added an Irish Catholic, a Presbyterian, a Jew, a Muslim from Turkestan, and a Buddhist from China, along with a Baptist missionary that I captured on the same trip. And in a very short while there wasn't a single living thing left in the cage!

The endemic weakness that accompanies the intensity of our more sacred concerns is a predilection for translating that intensity into intolerance, aggression, and violence. In this lies the seriousness of humor. The barbarous chronicle of inquisitions, heresy trials, witch-hunts, book-burnings, religious persecutions, political impris-onments, holy wars, and even acts of genocide—justified by the most respected elements of society and sanctified by pious interests—is sufficient testimony to the stark possibilities of sincerity without humor. Truth without laughter, and the sacred apart from the comic, are easily twisted into a perverse self-caricature. For example, it is difficult to imagine people who have a profound sense of humor in relation to their own most ultimate convictions participating in the burning of other people at the stake—as in John Calvin's Geneva—because of a failure to subscribe to a certain formulation of the doctrine of the Trinity!

The same debility besets the radical enthusiast of whatever persuasion who, in fanatical certainty over the righteousness of a cause, zealously pursues some grand program or vision. Whether a fiery exponent of Marxism, democracy, socialism, free enterprise, nationalism, minority rights, or military preparedness, the predispo-sition of the advocate—revolutionary, reactionary, or moderate—is to absolutize some scheme for saving the world and rectifying the ills of society. Ideologies, like religious dogmas, have a high level of missionary, and often military, zeal but a low level of comic awareness.

There is a marked affinity between religious absolutism, ideological dogmatism, and political tyranny. All share in the attempted abolition of humor in relation to themselves. A common trait of dictators, revolutionaries, and ecclesiastical authoritarians alike is the refusal both to laugh at themselves and to permit others to laugh at them. Charles de Gaulle once threatened a Parisian cartoonist—whose specialty was caricaturing the French president—with imprisonment by invoking a law instituted in the time of Napoleon. In totalitarian countries, humor and satire directed at the official ideology are the nearest equivalents to treason. Humorists who turn wit and wisdom in the direction of the functionaries and policies of the ascendant regime are open to the charge of unpatriotic, if not subversive, behavior—as in the religious sphere they are open to the charge of heresy or blasphemy.

In Stalinist Russia, comedies were permitted and even encouraged by the government. But they were of a certain type, namely, comedies that targeted capitalistic, imperialistic, democratic countries and that reinforced Leninist-Stalinist viewpoints. It was only in the less repressive and more liberal atmosphere, however modest, which entered after the death of Stalin that comedy and humor were permitted greater room to breathe. The Soviet magazine *Crocodil* signaled the change in 1953 by running a full-page advertisement for the best political joke, satire, or anecdote of the year. The promised award for the winning entry: "A free trip to Siberia."

A part of the pretension of orthodoxies of whatever sort is the claim to have elevated themselves beyond the requirements of humor. Such an exemption from the qualifications of humor, however, is equivalent to the claim to have transcended the human condition, to have become "as God," knowing in some final sense the difference between good and evil. Various attempts have been made historically to minimize the human element in matters of fundamental concern, and thereby the necessity for the comic perspective, through dogmatic positions and infallibilist presumptions. But like the proud who stumble in their moment of glory, or the foolish whose disguises fool no one but themselves, the very claim to have risen above the finiteness and fallibility of human nature is itself comic-pathetic and in its consequences so often tragic. In this sense, far from humor being a sign of the fall or of a trespass upon some holy ground, the absence of humor signifies the pride symbolized by the fall, and comedy a reminder of paradise lost. Humor acknowledges that "we see in a mirror dimly" (1 Cor. 13:12), and that we "know in part" and "prophesy in part." The alternative to humor is arrogance and idolatry.

The criterion by which one judges the importance an individual attaches to something is not necessarily the degree of unwillingness to laugh about it, to make it the grist of comedy or the target of puns and jokes. While such an attitude has been a common prejudice surrounding our most beloved opinions and convictions, it is the mark of pseudo-seriousness—in fact, the mark of what often becomes an inhuman and inhumane seriousness. Seriousness is human; it is the seriousness of this or that human being. Insofar as we remember our humanity, the play of humor is not irreverent or irresponsible but a moral and spiritual necessity. Without humor we become something less, not more, than human. We become not more divine but more demonic.

Though the playfulness of humor may jar our Calvinistic-Puritan-Capitalistic sensitivities, seriousness alone is stultifying and creates its own sterile forms of bondage, as well as violent forms of oppression. We need not only to be serious about certain things, but to laugh, to laugh even at our seriousness, to laugh at the things about which we become so serious and in which we become so seriously involved. We cannot be dead serious about law, for instance, without suffocating the spirit of the law in the process—as the natural history of legalism abundantly demonstrates. In George Santayana's words,

Where the spirit of comedy has departed, company becomes constraint, reserve eats up the spirit, and people fall into a penurious melancholy in their scruple to be always exact, sane, and reasonable. . . . Yet irony pursues these enemies of comedy, and for fear of wearing a mask for a moment they are hypocrites all their lives.[3]

Seriousness also intensifies anxiety. As long as one is completely immersed in and therefore circumscribed, defined, and determined by the little drama of the finite self, its opinions and situations, everything is quite sober and serious. A hushed mood of pontifical gravity and solemnity prevails, and trespassers on this holy ground must be punished, crucified, or beaten off. The comic perception, however, no matter how brief the glimmer, is itself an emancipation from the prison house of the self, its opinions and its situations. One is free to laugh. And in that freedom, life opens up to a different light and a larger perspective.

"High" and "Low" Laughter

Not any laughter will serve the purposes of humor, to be sure, as is well illustrated in the epitaph for the notorious Billy the Kid provided by his nemesis and biographer, Sheriff Pat Garrett: "Those who knew him best will tell you that in his most savage and dangerous moods his face always wore a smile. He ate and laughed, drank and laughed, rode and laughed, talked and laughed, fought and laughed—and killed and laughed."[4] This gives some credence to the common suggestion that laughter is born of aggression and antagonism. Certainly executions, lynching parties, torture chambers, and the like have always provided their own sadistic merriment. Nero, we may presume, laughed as well as fiddled while Rome burned. The laughter of the mob at the crucifixion of Jesus was of this baser sort: "He saved others, he cannot save himself." Laughter per se is hardly a reliable indicator of the comic spirit. Laughter can be arrogant, taunting, scornful, contemptuous, sneering, vulgar, cruel, nervous, giddy, hysterical, malicious, bitter, and insane. Laughter, for that matter, may also be the result of tickling and laughing gas.

Aristotle distinguished between a "liberal" and an "illiberal" laughter. Surely an illiberal laughter has effects opposite to those that Konrad Lorenz sees humor as encouraging. Rather than harmlessly releasing aggression, laughter may serve as the tool of aggression, and even incite it, as teasing schoolchildren and skillful propagandists know very well. Or instead of developing a larger perspective and a humbler posture, laughter may be used to reinforce one's prejudices and sense of superiority, as sexist and racist and Polish jokes do quite successfully.

To some extent we are thrown back on Anthony Ludovici's theory that the smile has its origin in the animal's baring its teeth as a threatening or threatened gesture, just as the handshake is credited with having its origin in a gesture that stopped hands and bodies short of a less happy collision.[5] If so, the smile is a significantly redirected expression that moves from hostility to friendliness, from the tension of strangers meeting to a relaxed atmosphere of congeniality. And the accompanying laughter likewise moves from aggression to acceptance and goodwill. On this line of interpretation an "illiberal" laughter is a laughter that moves back toward the original baring of the teeth. It is laughter retrogressing to the growl and the snarl.

Laughter may also be used in excusing oneself by "laughing it off," where change or restitution might otherwise be in order. It may be a way of refusing to look candidly at oneself, so that instead of unmasking pride and pretension they may only be masked more effectively.

Laughter, too, can become an easy path of escape from intellectual labor, moral accountability, and profound commitment. It can degenerate into a frivolous diversion from the tortuous and seemingly intractable issues that confront us. And laughter can simply be trivial, dealing as many comics do with clever gags and word tricks, witticisms of the moment that are quickly forgotten because they do not touch us at the core of our being. They provide only a convenient diversion, a false sense of security.

Because of the variety of illiberal forms of laughter, it has been easy for sensitive souls to see it as a dangerous and volatile gas that must be tightly bottled up. Plato rejects a comic art that so easily arouses the "rebellious principle" in the populace, especially at public festivals, and counsels the guardians of his ideal state not to indulge in laughter or to play the clown. Ecclesiastics have been known to have similar misgivings over the value of laughter, usually preferring to keep it at a respectable distance from holy things, if not to eliminate it altogether, after the manner of the Rule of Saint Benedict: "As for coarse jests and idle words or words that lead to laughter, these we condemn with a perpetual ban." Even Baudelaire argued that there is a "violent" and "satanic" element in laughter, and that it is so closely associated with feelings of pride, superiority, and defiance that it may be said to be "intimately linked with the accident of an ancient Fall."

Though such examples of uneasiness about the comic could be multiplied indefinitely, and though many forms of "fallen" laughter do serve to support such views, the humorist does not trade in any and all sorts of laughter. The laughter of humor *may* strike out at persons or circumstances as a substitute for more violent alternatives and as a harmless escape-valve for tensions and frustrations. And it may do so particularly when the laughter is justified by the object—for example, laughter at a haughty individual caught in a ridiculous pose, or at someone whose pretensions have suddenly been exposed. Laughter at an oppressor, similarly, is a way of converting the grimace of suffering into a smile. Or the laughter of an inferior toward a superior is a way of momentarily reversing and equalizing their relationship. Such uses of laughter are not "fallen" but are aimed at a restoration of balance and a renewed sense of dignity and fair play. Comic *justice* is served.

But at its highest, the laughter of humor is a laughter in which, if one laughs at others, one is also willing to laugh at oneself. Even in laughing at others one vicariously laughs at oneself, for humor sees all as sharing in a common human nature and the common predicaments, embarrassments, and temptations of life. The humorist laughs *with* and not just *at* other people. The laughter of humor is thus able to function relative to those things which we may hold dear and cherish, including ourselves, as well as all those things which others, in ways that may seem foolish and therefore funny to us, hold dear and cherish. Humor is not aimed solely outside the self or the in-group. It circles back upon our own postures and claims, foibles and failings. Humor is like the bauble carried by the fool in medieval and renaissance Christendom which might be used to mock and caricature others or simply to hit other people over the head, but which also bore a likeness of the fool in comic miniature.

Once this step is made, humor is opened up to sympathy and goodwill. Those who are able to include themselves in their laughter are also able to include others in their generosity. A humor that heretofore has moved within the context of comic release and comic justice now moves within a context of empathy and kindred feeling. Humor is freed to become the humor of humility and compassion.

Such a comic sensitivity is much more than a keen wit, quick repartee, ingenious word-play, or the wag's talent for making others laugh—all of which might take place completely outside a sense of humor with respect to oneself, as an examination of the biographies of certain well-known clowns and comics would clearly reveal. The ability to be funny and get laughs has nothing directly to do with gaining a comic understanding of one's own existence, or of human existence as such. The technique of the comic twist is not identical to the art of humor. One may make mirth daily for the admiring masses yet not necessarily have succeeded in personally existentializing the comic spirit and perspective.

Humor at its best is a comic sensitivity in this more mature, internalized form. The perspective it provides is a perspective on one's own life, not just other people's lives, and on the whole of life, not just occasional and peripheral moments. The humorist, as the specialist in humor, is therefore to be distinguished from the satirist, the ironist, the wit, and the comic. The humorist may use satire, irony, wit, and a variety of comic devices, yet speak and act out of a more profound spirit and a more all-embracing vision. In humor dwells the truth of Kierkegaard's dictum "The more thoroughly and substantially a human being exists, the more he will discover the comical. Even one who has merely conceived a great plan toward accomplishing something in the world will discover it."[6] The wit and the comic may offer entertainment and diversion, along with a means of elevating ourselves at the expense of others, but the humorist offers a kind of salvation. The laughter of humor has a redemptive quality.

The art of humor is, however, forever encountering misunderstandings. The situation is hardly improved by multiplying the number of stand-up comics in nightclubs or the percentage of comedies in cinema, television, and theater offerings. It is probably worsened. When humor is so commonly associated in the popular mind with "illiberal" and immature forms of laughter, humor is that much more easily prevented from becoming internalized and mature and from addressing us in the totality of our lives.

Professional interpretations of the humorist's art are not always helpful, and sometimes they are quite misleading. Even Al Capp—who, if he was not being facetious, should have known better—stated baldly, "All comedy is based on man's delight in man's inhumanity to man . . . and this has been the basis of all the comedy I have created." The joke or comic performance or cartoon strip portrays people who are uglier, dumber, poorer, hungrier, lonelier, or grumpier than we are, so that we may come away enjoying our superiority and congratulating ourselves on our greater good fortune.[7] It isn't true, of course, not even of Al Capp's comedy. Daisy Mae was uncommonly beautiful. Li'l Abner's physique was the envy of every red-blooded American body-builder. Mammy Yocum, despite having the stature of a pygmy, had superhuman strength and a firm control of almost every situation. Other Capp characters, such as Lem and Luke Scragg, were definitely beneath us, burning down orphanages to get some light for reading their comic books, and in other like ways endearing themselves. But they also turned out to be better than most of us in dutifully asking their father's permission to perform their dastardly deeds. On the other hand, Mammy Yocum tended to be bossy. Daisy Mae, for all her charms, was almost totally unsuccessful in gaining the attention, let alone the attentions, of Li'l Abner. Li'l Abner, while seemingly a hunk of ultramasculinity, had no interest in kissing anyone but his mother and his pig. In other words, comic characters are on the average not inferior to us but both better and worse than we are, and a part of the comedy they present has to do with the incongruities this makes possible and the awkwardnesses that result. Comic characters mirror in striking form our own existence.

Even though no less (and no more) an authority than Thomas Hobbes may be quoted in support of the theory, "Laughter is a sudden glory arising at the sight of an inferior," it is a garbage collector's view of the comic sensibility. Everything is thrown away but the trash. Humor would hardly be worth devoting a career to if this were all laughter amounted to. It would also hardly be worth burning anyone at the stake over.

Another common misunderstanding of humor is that it is basically trivial. Gordon Allport refers to the psychological function of humor as that of helping "to integrate personality by disposing of all conflicts that do not really matter."[8] Reinhold Niebuhr, writing in the period of disillusionment following World War II, argued, "Laughter is our reaction to immediate incongruities and those which do not affect us essentially. Faith is the only possible response to the ultimate incongruities of existence which threaten the very meaning of our life. . . . Man's very position in the universe is incongruous. That is the problem of faith, and not of humour."[9]

Yet this cannot be true, for in the first instance this would mean that somehow human beings were not free to laugh relative to the fundamental incongruities of their nature—a minor difficulty that would soon be dispensed with by but a single small child finding humor in such incongruities and laughing. In the second instance, this would hardly answer the difficulty that much of "man's inhumanity to man" historically is the result of some faith, some vision or ideal, that has been taken absolutely and with absolute seriousness. When one considers all the "good" that has been done to the human race in the name of one faith or another, faith has considerable incongruities of its own to worry about. If humor without faith is in danger of dissolving into cynicism and despair, faith without humor is in danger of turning into arrogance and intolerance. Faith without humor is itself an incongruity, for it is inevitably the faith of this or that finite and conditioned group of human beings—as the humorist is quick to point out.

A similar misunderstanding is that humor concerns itself only with issues that are basically unimportant to us. Humor plays in the relative safety and irrelevance of the circumference of our lives. In Harold Watts's words, "It is the trick of comedy to confirm all our superficial judgments; it must make us ignore those which we regard as profound and eternal."[10] While this is no doubt true of some comedy and humor, it is not true of all. In fact, quite the opposite is the case in the most mature and internalized expressions of the comic vision. At first sight the comic sense may seem inappropriate to the seriousness of our most fundamental problems and persuasions. Yet it is precisely here that humor is most needed. It is least needed on the periphery of our lives. And to restrict it to such marginality is to offer a self-fulfilling prophecy: Humor is trivial and superficial.

As Aristotle reminded the disputants of his day, quoting Gorgias: "Humor is the only test of gravity, and gravity of humor. For a subject which will not bear raillery is suspicious; and a jest which will not bear serious examination is false wit." Comic protagonists are often *socially* marginal, a position that gives them a certain immunity in the precarious business of dealing humorously with matters others hold very dear. But they do not therefore deal only in marginal issues. The philosophy of the humorist may be put quite succinctly: Anything that is serious is worthy of humorous consideration.

Nietzsche—though not a model witness to these matters—in the same passage of *Zarathustra* in which he exclaimed that he "would only believe in a god who could dance" went on to identify Satan as the one who is "serious, thorough, profound and solemn." As false god and antigod, it is Satan who is "the spirit of gravity, through whom all things fall."

Three Levels of Humor

If one were to put these arguments in more systematic fashion, three levels of humor might be identified. Humorists are not particularly enthusiastic about systems and charts, being more inclined to parody or frustrate them than espouse them. As Edwards remarked to Johnson in James Boswell's *Life of Samuel Johnson*, "I have tried too in my time to be a philosopher, but, I don't know how, cheerfulness was always breaking in." Still, some initial map is essential for understanding humor—as it is here being interpreted—and for suggesting a more adequate frame of reference than is commonly given.

From a mythic standpoint, humor may be said to function on three levels, corresponding symbolically to the themes of paradise, paradise lost, and paradise regained. Humor is a playful return to a past innocence and unity, a reflection and release of present tensions and contradictions, or a recovery on a higher level of lost innocence and unity.

The laughter of paradise. At the simplest and most innocent level, humor is a form of playing for the sake of playing—whether with words, concepts, objects, situations, or persons. It is one of the ways human beings frolic, play the fool, indulge in silliness, act with childlike abandon, and deliver themselves to the caprice of the instant. Through puns and tall tales and absurdities, we enter that freedom which resists being fixed in rigid categories or sterile reasonableness or wooden eternal appropriateness. Like the play of little children, humor in this sense is a sheer "waste" of time and energy. It is a leap into that "wild and carefree, inexhaustible joy of life invincible."[11]

A book of elephant jokes compiled by a public school student contains the following prefatory note by the publisher: "Warning! Practically no parents will think elephant jokes are funny." An example: "What did Tarzan say when he saw the elephants coming? 'Here come the elephants.' What did Jane say? 'Here come the plums' (She's color blind)."[12] There is here no antagonism toward elephants being vented, no sense of inferiority or superiority to ponderous pachyderms, no anxiety over the prospect of being run down by a herd of wild elephants, no catharsis for elephant complexes. Nor is there necessarily any implied sexism or tension between the sexes. The joke is just plain fun. One is enjoying being nonsensical for the sake of being nonsensical in a refusal to make sense or make progress or make money all the time. The "weightier matters of the law"—and of elephants— are set aside, and another world, the world of playfulness, is entered through the peculiar freedom of humor. It is the world of innocence prior to the knowledge of good and evil, outside of shame and guilt, where taboos do not exist and where there are neither things important nor things unimportant, sacred nor profane—the world biblically represented by the original innocence of Adam and Eve.

In such a world everything becomes, in a sense, unimportant and profane, and therefore fair game as the object of laughter—a thesis which *Monty Python's Flying Circus* has used quite successfully. Yet in another sense everything becomes playfully important and in-discriminately endowed with holiness—as in the *Batman* television farces, where Robin's exclamations announced the most mundane variety of things as holy: "Holy smoke rings," "Holy caffeine," "Holy syllogisms," "Holy hypothesis," "Holy jelly beans." Such humor is most open to the charge of being trivial, frivolous, and irresponsible. Yet this misses the point of comic banter, for the distinctions between significant and trivial, serious and frivolous, holy and unholy, are not available. They have been set aside in the recollected laughter of children.

The laughter of paradise lost. Humor is not all innocence, however. At a more sophisticated level, it stands more self-consciously in the midst of conflict and anxiety, success and failure, faith and doubt. It is not so much a humor that lays aside the tensions of life in a holiday of innocence as a humor that moves within those tensions in comic reflection of them. It is, consequently, the comic mode that corresponds mythically with paradise lost. And its laughter proceeds from the Adamic "knowledge of good and evil."

Here we begin to encounter laughter as a means of expressing frustration, fear, and antagonism. W.C. Fields is credited with saying that no one who hates children can be all bad. And much of Fields's humor expressed the hostilities we often feel toward children and dogs and salespeople and spouses. There *are* things about children that can be irritating at times. And laughter with respect to those persons or situations that we do not like is a means of disposing of matters symbolically. Whether or not anything is actually disposed of other than our immediate irritations, we feel better about it. The humorist provides us with a ritual triumph. We even manage to enjoy, through the magical transformations of humor, the very sources of our irritations.

Raised to a higher plane, such humor becomes a means of dispensing a kind of poetic justice. Much laughter is *justified*, as in the proverbial example of the proud man falling on a banana peel. Humor has an ethical dimension to it which fastens on hypocrisy and injustice. It delights in humbling the mighty, counterbalancing inequities, and reducing conflicts. Charles Chaplin was much criticized for his comic parody of Adolf Hitler and Nazi anti-Semitism in *The Great Dictator* (1940), and he himself had misgivings about the film when the actual fate of Europe and the Jews became a horrible reality. Still, the central concern of the film was clearly comic justice, as Chaplin played the lookalike roles of a German dictator and an oppressed Jewish barber. The dictator, ranting and parading about, or playing with his balloon globe of the world, was exposed as the twisted fool that he was, while the harassed and homeless Jewish barber was revealed as the genuinely human and courageous individual that he was. And in the final scene the Jewish barber, fleeing toward the border, is mistaken for the dictator and whisked away to a Nazi rally, where he delivers an appeal for the cessation of the hatred and madness "he" had initiated.

At this level, humor also begins to come to terms more directly with the ambiguities and ambivalences of human existence. Humor plays, for example, with all the awkwardnesses of our self-conscious animality as thinking creatures: flesh and spirit, sex and love, impulse and reason. Hence all the jokes about food and sex and foolishness. Usually human awkwardnesses are presented in their least distressing though perhaps most embarrassing forms: a seat collapses under the dignity of the portly major; the queen's slip is showing; the preacher's false teeth fall out at the climax of a sermon; the ranting politician gets a pie in the face; a lovemaking scene is interrupted by the sudden cave-in of the bed. Yet these minor awkwardnesses point to a deeper level of awkwardness.

There is an intrinsic awkwardness about human nature and its position in the cosmos as such. The glory and pathos of the human situation to which Pascal referred so poignantly in his *Pensées* has its humorous side as well. It is upon the tensions generated by this "existential predicament" that humor now draws its energies. Instead of leaping out of the "predicament" in a temporary amnesia of innocence, it remains to confront the situation comically. Humor in fact becomes a reminder of this awkwardness, especially for those inclined to forget it (its *iconoclastic* or *prophetic* function, which it shares with satire and irony). And it offers a means of accepting this awkwardness and coping with it (its *cathartic* or *purgative* function).

These two movements of humor are readily illustrated in the peculiar freedom available to court jesters to profane the sacred person and rule of the king, to mock the pomp of royalty, to transgress the code of the court, even now and then to proclaim themselves king. On the one hand, jesters provided kings with a comic perspective on themselves and their role as finite rulers. On the other hand, jesters served as scapegoats for the anger and frustration of kings, while in turn also providing the court with a relatively harmless avenue for expressing animosity or opposition to the throne.

At this level, too, humor begins to come to terms with absurdity, evil, suffering, and death, and it does so in part by playfully refusing to take these features of human experience with absolute seriousness and thereby to be controlled or destroyed by them. Laughter is not all gaiety and mirth. It may also express the struggle against the hard and harsh side of life—the "thorns and thistles" or "slings and arrows" of our common destiny and individual fortune. In it bursts forth the will to live, the courage to be.

Such a humor may function, modestly, along the lines of James Thurber's reaction to a young woman's offhand remark: "We are not going to hide our heads in the sand like kangaroos." Said Thurber, "This was just what my harassed understanding and tortured spirits needed. I was, it is not too much to say, saved by the twisted and inspired simile, and whenever I think I hear the men coming with the stretcher or the subpoena, I remember those kangaroos with their heads in the sand, and I am ready to face anything again."[13]

The same capacity of the comic spirit is more profoundly visible in the remarkable phenomenon of Jewish humor, for the Jews, like the American blacks, have developed a genius for comedy in the midst of very tragic histories. It is hardly a coincidence that a high percentage of comedians in the United States, especially relative to their proportions in the population statistics, are Jewish or black. Humor is not only possible in relation to the more superficial and inconsequential incongruities of life. As gallows humor or concentration-camp humor will attest, it may also express a certain heroic defiance in the face of life's most crushing defeats, an unquenchable nobility of spirit that refuses to permit a given fate or oppressor to have the last word—to be absolute. The human spirit has not been utterly vanquished. The will to live and the determination to continue the struggle, or the faith that the struggle will be continued, has not been finally conquered. Where there is humor there is still hope.

The laughter of paradise regained. There is, however, another level of humor, though it may be achieved only rarely. It is prefigured in the laughter of innocence, yet it is not identical with it. It is the laughter that comes beyond good and evil, rather than before it. It is the laughter of maturity, the laughter in the freedom of a higher innocence and unity, that corresponds mythically to paradise regained. One has now become free in the fullest sense to laugh.

It is to such a level that Wylie Sypher alludes when he speaks of the "radiant peak of 'high comedy'" where "laughter is qualified by tolerance, and criticism is motivated by a sympathy that comes only from wisdom." A victory is won over our absurdities "at a cost of humility . . . and in a spirit of charity and enlightenment . . . without despair, without rancor, as if human blunders were seen from a godlike distance."[14] Such a magnanimous humor is not easily realized, but it should not therefore be discounted or ignored. It is, in a sense, the final goal and fulfillment of humor. Humor moves from playful innocence through truth and justice to humility and compassion.

The distinctive feature of this form of humor is that it is generated not by inner tension but by an inner harmony. It does not reflect conflict so much as resolution. Clearly this is the most dynamic and self-contained humor, for it proceeds not from a position of weakness and turmoil but from a position of strength. It is like the difference between the laughter of adversaries and the laughter among friends. Whether one sees the context of such humor in terms of faith, trust, serenity, or affirmation of life, the laughter it produces comes from a profound sense of security rather than insecurity. It does not come from the spleen. It presupposes faith in some sacred order or depth-dimension of being, some common basis of worth and dignity, at the same time that it represents a persistent unwillingness to dogmatize its understanding of that faith and worth.

There is therefore an intimate relationship between humor and compassion. Instead of moving only in the direction of a laughter at others and their faults and foibles or supposed inferiorities, humor moves toward a laughter that accepts others in spite of their differences. Since it is not grounded in a nervous insecurity, it does not need to be self-protective and self-assertive. It is therefore capable of becoming, in the purest sense, the humor of love. The element of judgment in humor (its prophetic, iconoclastic function) passes over into mercy.

In the Christian context this passing over is seen, in fact, as the result of a prior mercy, a divine grace which has bestowed forgiveness and acceptance upon those who do not warrant it, either by virtue of their own righteousness or rightness. Such forgiveness being neither deserved nor earned, the recipient of grace is freed to accept others in a common mercy and compassion. In this freedom humor is able to go beyond dispensing judgment upon the follies and hypocrisies of others and dispenses, as it were, a kind of divine grace.

Grace, as Northrop Frye has argued, is an important theme in the most mature comedies. Comic grace is grace both in the sense of the graceful courtier or gracious host or hostess and in the sense of a long-suffering, forgiving, and reconciling divine grace. The humorist, though capable of very pointed criticism and of putting people in bold relief, leads the way finally to acceptance rather than rejection. Instead of the distances between people being enlarged and hardened, they are reduced and softened. In Shakespearean comedy, for example, as Frye notes,

when we find Falstaff invited to the final feast in *The Merry Wives*, Caliban reprieved [in *The Tempest*], attempts made to mollify Malvolio [in *Twelfth Night*], and Angelo [*Measure for Measure*] and Parolles [*All's Well That Ends Well*] allowed to live down their disgrace, we are seeing a fundamental principle of comedy at work. The tendency of the comic society to include rather than exclude is the reason for the traditional importance of the parasite, who has no business to be at the final festival but is nevertheless there.[15]

There is a kind of recovery of childlikeness in this, for children have the remarkable capacity to forgive and forget over matters that in the adult world become permanent grudges. Children can have the worst quarrel of which they are capable and in a few hours—or minutes—are back playing together as if every moment were a new moment and nothing quite so important as play. Because children are not given to absolutizing themselves and their situations, reconciliation comes easily and the festival can begin once more.

Here too those other virtues of the child are recovered: spontaneity, immediacy, lightheartedness, playfulness, naturalness. To be sure, a distinction must be drawn between childlikeness and childishness. Many adults quite successfully kill their former childlikeness but in the process kill also the possibility of a mature childlikeness. Much of what passes for adulthood is therefore not maturity but an advanced and hardened stage of adolescence. The adolescent imagines that adulthood is achieved through a process of forgetting and destroying one's former identity as a child, but maturity is reached by becoming once again—as an adult—like the child.

Joseph Campbell put it a little differently: "It is the gift of immaturity itself, which has enabled us to retain in our best, most human moments the capacity for play. . . . It is, in fact, only those who have failed, one way or another [to preserve this gift] in their manhood or womanhood, who become our penny-dreadfuls, our gorillas and baboons."[16] The world ruled by seriousness alone grows old, faded, wooden, rigid, lifeless. The grave world is indeed the world of the grave. But the world in the reign of the comic spirit grows young again—lively, vital, creative, dancing, joyful. It is a world that is guarded not, like Eden, by some angel of judgment with a flaming sword, but by the high priests of comedy who invite all to come in who will lay down their rifles and rattles, their poses and posturings, their masks and trumpetings. It is a world which, as Johan Huizinga said of poetry, "lies beyond seriousness, on that more primitive and original level where the child, the animal, the savage and the seer belong, in the region of dream, enchantment, ecstasy, laughter."[17]

Chapter 2

Jester to the Kingdoms of Earth

Evil prevails where laughter is not known.
—Iglulik Eskimo saying[1]

At the court of King Alboin of Lombardy in the sixth century A.D. there suddenly appeared a creature named Bertoldo. Court records describe him as being ugly, dwarfed, and deformed, with carrot-colored hair. He marched directly to the throne, and brashly seated himself beside King Alboin. The king demanded to know who he was, where he came from, and by what authority he dared enter the king's court uninvited and sit beside the throne. Bertoldo replied: "I am a man. I was born the night my mother bore me. And the world is my country."[2]

One of the redeeming features of ancient and medieval monarchies was that they recognized that a king needs a court jester, not only to be the scapegoat for court jokes but also to play the role of the king in comic caricature. A part of the function of jesters was to make kings laugh and to offer themselves as objects of laughter, but it was also their function to make kings laugh at themselves and to permit others (indirectly) to laugh at them. To be sure, jesters, with their comical appearance and manner and speech, were engaged and retained as a form of entertainment. Yet in their entertaining way they represented a spirit and perspective that stood outside the laws and jurisdiction of any particular earthly kingdom. They wandered into courts as people from another world, and to them the world was their country.

It was hardly an accident of history that kings permitted such deformed, dwarfed, and "demented" figures as Bertoldo to intrude on the royal presence. The elevation of the royal person and rule to a godlike station required the comic person and mock rule of the jester in order to preserve that delicate balance of power on either side of which were the pitfalls of tyranny and anarchy. If the king did not admit the jester to his court, the door was open to absolutism and despotism. But if the jester's iconoclasm became too successful, the door was open to social disruption and political chaos.

The jester thus represented the humorous qualification of all human orders and enterprises. The kingdom was served by a comic king who stood outside the earthly authority of the monarchy and in tension with it. The jester was a creature without rank and power, from whom the king had, it would seem, nothing to fear. Yet as a fool, and because a fool, the jester was capable of playing a prophetic role and representing a larger spirit and higher wisdom.

Truth-teller

In Roman times it was the custom of returning conquerors or heroes to carry a slave in their chariot as a symbolic acknowledgment that they were human beings and not a threat to the power of the gods. It was the duty of this *servulus* to exhort warriors not to be overly proud of their victory, lest they be guilty of what the Greeks would have called *hubris*. They were to be honored by the populace as they rode to the Capitol, but abuses (*molestie*) in the form of taunts and jests were also permitted. In ancient Rome it was also the practice for a jester (*mimus*) to follow in the funeral procession of the emperor to provide diversion from the somberness of the occasion and even to mimic the dead emperor. Suetonius mentions a *mimus* named Faco, who accompanied Vespasian's funeral procession dressed as the emperor, mimicking even such traits as his presumed miserliness by asking bystanders how much the funeral was costing him.[3]

Records of jesters in the English monarchy go back to the court of Edmund Ironside (eleventh century), and for the French line to Hugh Capet (tenth century). Though introduced primarily as a diversion, in a later time jesters were often to become quite influential figures as advisers and confidants. Edward IV had his Scoggins; Henry VIII his

Will Sommers and John Heywood; Queen Elizabeth her Richard Tarleton; Charles II his Tom Killegrew; Henry III (of France) his Chicot. Not all kings, it is true, had jesters. According to one account no jester of any consequence was known to have been retained by the court of William Rufus, "the king, indeed, hardly needing one; for he was accustomed not only to make his own jokes, but to laugh louder at them than any other person!"

In a sense, the jester provided the king with a comic alter ego, a less serious, more human, and more flexible self to step into. The jester was the king's symbolic twin—as is suggested in the belief registered by Rabelais in *Gargantua and Pantagruel* that "those who wear the crown and scepter were born under the same sign as those who wear the cap and bells." In the king-as-jester—or jester-as-king—there was a softening of the contradiction in the person of the king as both sacred ruler and mortal human being. In the form of the jester, the king was prevented from pretending to be what he was not and permitted to be what he really was: a human being like everyone else, who participated with all his subjects in the frailties and follies of the human condition. The freedom of the court jester to violate all the proprieties and taboos of royalty, to flaunt pomposity and decorum, was vicariously experienced by the king as his own freedom, his personal emancipation from the rigid confines of his role and the loftiness of his responsibility. He was able to step out from behind the mask and costume of his official self and station into his other self. What Wylie Sypher has said of the function of the carnival may be said of the role of the jester:

Those in the thrall of carnival come out for a moment from behind the façade of their "serious" selves, the façade required by their vocation. When they emerge from this façade, they gain a new perspective upon their official selves and thus, when they again retire behind their usual *personae*, they are more conscious of the duplicity of their existence.[4]

Through jesters, kings preserved both their sanity and their humanity.

At the same time, the court and populace were provided with a relatively harmless—though not necessarily ineffectual—avenue for venting animosity and discontent. The behavior of the jester was an instance of what Max Gluckman has called "rituals of rebellion." "Every social system is a field of tension, full of ambivalence, of cooperation and contrasting struggle."[5] To act out these conflicts is a way of acknowledging that the conflicts exist and of permitting a certain amount of rebellion to exist. But because the antagonisms are played out, and especially when played out comically, they are prevented from being destructive of the order and authority within which they move. Yet they are capable of making a difference.

In certain African kingship systems, rather than a fool playing the role of king, the king was required annually to play the fool. The king, who by virtue of rank and power was elevated above all other members of the tribe, made this periodic descent from the highest to the lowest station, thus reversing and overturning his normal status. He dressed in rags, walked unescorted through the village, and begged for food. The members of the tribe, over which the king held sway through the rest of the year, were permitted to taunt and insult him. And the king was supposed to talk gibberish as if he were the village imbecile. In this way the social hierarchy was inverted for a season. The king moved from the top of the social order to the bottom, while his subjects were permitted to "lord" it over him. The sacred person and role of the king were thus ritually profaned, rendering the inequities and rigidities of the social system more tolerable. (A similar custom prevailed at the Roman Saturnalia, when slaves took the role of their masters, and masters were to obey their slaves.)

The symbolic kinship between king and fool is further evident in the fact that the jester was often the one member of the court who had the most immediate access to the king, requiring no special permission or announcement, as if the jester were the king's shadow. Though the jester was a shadow that could be beheaded, this eventuality was remarkably rare, considering the amount of freedom this peculiar station afforded. For example, the jester was one through whom difficult news might be passed when no one else dared tell the king the truth—as in the case of the defeat of the French fleet of Philip by the English fleet of Edward III. When the task of informing Philip was given to his jester, the jester began pacing about muttering curses on the cowardly English sailors who were afraid to jump in the sea when so many brave French sailors did so so readily!

An important aspect of the jester's role was therefore that of truth-teller. The social distance between king and jester was so great—like that between adult and child—that the jester could stand closer to the king, and deal with him more directly and straightforwardly, than others who might constitute a more obvious threat to royal authority and power. This paradoxical classification gave the jester a kind of freedom and license that other humans did not have—even the king, who was still bound by the dignity and expectation of his role. Thus in a court full of flattery, elegant manners, elaborate protocol, and pretty speeches, the jester was the one capable of the greatest directness, honesty, and candor.

One may cite the case of the Chinese emperor responsible for completing the Great Wall, Ch'in Shih Huang Ti, who had a court jester named Yu Sze. After the 1,500 miles of wall had been constructed at great expense and with considerable hardship for the tens of thousands of laborers, the emperor decided to have it painted. All knew this would mean an even greater expenditure of resources and lives, yet none of the court advisers had the courage to question the emperor's wishes—except for Yu Sze, who so successfully ridiculed the proposal that the emperor abandoned it.

Jesters were notoriously bold in their ridicule, criticism, and advocacy. And even though their remarks and insinuations might be dismissed as "fool's license," they had the potential for wielding considerable political and social power. As one early commentator, John Fuller, said of Richard Tarleton: "He told the Queen [Elizabeth I] more of her faults than most of her chaplains." Jesters, because of their social marginality and their wit and humor were the ones most able to say or do what for anyone else might result in imprisonment or execution. When Henry VIII and his court were celebrating the much disputed conferral of the title "Defender of the Faith," the king's jester shook his head in mocking disapproval and said, "Let thou and I defend one another, and let faith alone to defend itself."[6]

Jesters served, therefore, what might be called a prophetic function. They did not necessarily claim any divine message or mission, but they moved in and out of the social and political orders of the day as if representing some higher order. Like the prophet Nathan before a King David that had schemed to get Bathsheba, Uriah's wife, the jester was able to enter the inner sanctum of the palace and tell the king an innocent story, the punch line of which was "Thou art the man."

In the Muslim world the paramount example is Nasr-ed-Din of the fourteenth century. Diminutive in stature and wearing a huge turban, he appeared at the court of the ruthless conqueror Timur, seeking employment. Timur said he would give him a job if he could answer a list of questions; if not, he would be executed. Nasr-ed-Din's responses so amused the emperor Timur that he accepted him into the court. Like all court jesters, he tended to be very bold in his speech, always walking the thin line between employment and execution. One day Timur saw his aging face in a barber's mirror and began to wail at the sight. The court politely wailed with him, including Nasr-ed-Din. After the emperor regained his composure, Nasr-ed-Din continued his loud lamentations. When Timur asked why he carried on so, Nasr-ed-Din sobbed, "You wept over just one glimpse of yourself. But I have to look at you all day!"

It is difficult for us to imagine at this point in time the degree to which fools were highly visible and almost commonplace individuals in ancient, medieval, and renaissance societies. They were found not only in king's castles but also at the tables of nobility, in the houses and bedchambers of the wealthy, and even at the side of popes, cardinals, bishops, and lesser prelates. A fool was part of the normal entourage of almost anyone of stature, a member of the household in a manner similar to a servant, yet in a world apart. Dwarfs and midgets in particular sometimes acted as companions to children in the combined role of playmate and servant. Fools were also found in traveling shows and festivals, processions and country fairs, taverns and brothels. And this prevalence of folly made the fool a familiar figure in the art, literature, drama, and moral treatises of the period.

But by the eighteenth century the fool had become increasingly out of fashion in the royal courts and among the aristocracy, being less suited to reformed, educated, and enlightened tastes. The fool's domain was reduced to the performing stage, traveling show, and country fair, where kindred spirits had always been. The more grotesque "freaks" were hidden away, to reemerge in nineteenth-century sideshows. Dwarfs could await the coming of the circus and the cinema. The demented and the retarded began to be cared for in the new social fashion of cloistering them in institutions.

Today individuals who formerly might have found employment as fools, and who give us some surviving link to the fool tradition, are now comic actors, comedians, clowns, mimes, poets and artists, circus performers, sideshow attractions, or residents of state asylums. There was a time, however—and it was a long time—when fools in one or another form had an important niche in society and played a significant social role. The fool was therefore a considerably more immediate and powerful symbol than today, when the remembrance of so tangible a figure belongs only to renaissance plays and history books.

The Religious Fool

Historically the fool has stood in a mocking relationship to spiritual as well as political kingdoms. And here too we find a peculiar priesthood. Among the Navaho, for example, in the night chant ceremony, the water god (*to ninili*) is impersonated in the sacred dance by a foolish figure dressed in rags and playing the buffoon. While the other masked dancers are intently and meticulously pursuing the intricate rhythms and patterns of the ceremony, the fool's function is to mimic the entire proceeding. Comically he exaggerates all the proper gestures and movements, or with mock determination attempts to follow the other dancers, but invariably gets everything wrong. The fool dances out of step, staggers, trips, and falls—to the delight of the audience. Sometimes he stumbles or leaps out of the prescribed arena, dashing into the crowd and indulging in pranks, taunts, and teasing. He wears a fox's tail, which frequently falls off and, though it lies at his feet, he scours the arena in search of what is in plain sight of everyone.[7]

This is a surprising kind of religious ritual. Here the comic profaning of the sacred, rather than following the sacred drama or being performed to one side in a more secular time and space, is incorporated into the rite itself. The dialectic of seriousness and laughter, of solemnity and playfulness, is openly enacted. In the special genius of this tribal rite, these two movements of the human spirit are openly juxtaposed and united. Both together are the authentic portrayal and expression of human nature and human feeling. Human beings are not only like the other nine masked dancers, perfectly executing the prescribed religious forms in a staid and stately manner. They are also like the tenth dancer. And it is the tenth dancer's ritual mission to introduce this other side of our existence, to admit it, accept it, enjoy it, and in fact encourage it. The whole person, as it were, dances before the gods.

In modern Haiti a similar phenomenon has taken the form of a good-natured ridicule of religious matters, as in the "catechism of the

Guede," in which Roman Catholic devotees, catechetical instructions, and ecclesiastical functionaries are parodied. At the end of a ceremony in honor of ancestral spirits (the Guede), the participants are commanded by the leader to form a line and are given a mock catechetical examination, the answers to which are facetiously or ludicrously phrased. Each answer qualifies the "catechumen" for some prestigious ecclesiastical, political, or military title. At the culmination of the examination the most unlikely candidate—perhaps a fat girl of jolly spirits—is acclaimed "Pope."[8] Such burlesque may seem to border on sacrilege, except that it is performed in a buoyant rather than malicious spirit for the common sport of all.

Of similar order were the three medieval festivals following Christmas: Holy Innocents Day, the Feast of Fools, and the Feast of Asses. On Holy Innocents Day (*festum puerorum*) the gravity and grandeur of the holy office of bishop was suspended in the appointment of a boy bishop. For one day the awesome authority and responsibility of the church was returned to the playful innocence of childhood, with the boy bishop officiating at a service in which the ecclesiastical positions and functions were assumed by children, concluding later with his bestowal of the episcopal blessing from the residence of the archbishop.

The Feast of Fools (*festum stultorum*) had less of the aura of innocence about it. In a period of reveling following Christmas, the inferior clergy burlesqued the offices and roles of their superiors. In many cases a "lord of misrule" was elected to supplant the holder of the *baculus* (wand of office), the installation occurring at Vespers during that portion of the Magnificat beginning "He has put down the mighty from their thrones, and exalted those of low degree [Luke 1:52]." In some instances this theme was elaborated to include also a "fool's pope." The Feast of Asses (*festum asinorum*) became yet another vehicle for comic profanation. As a festival commemorating Mary's flight into Egypt, an ass was ridden into the sanctuary by a young girl carrying an infant boy. With the ass and its riders standing beside the altar, a mass was sung in dog-Latin rhyme, with priest and congregation braying the refrain: "Haw, Sir Ass, he-haw."[9]

The fool has had a long association with the ass. More than any other animal the ass has served as mascot and symbol of the fool tradition. Donkeys and burros have been ridden or accompanied by comic figures from early Greek miming to modern clowning. In Greek processions one might have seen mimes riding in or following the donkey cart of comedy. In the Middle Ages, fools were depicted with asses' ears—an association drawn upon in Erasmus' *Praise of Folly*. The English clown Grimaldi sang one of his most popular songs, "Me and My Neddy," astride a hobby ass. The fact that Jesus was represented as riding into Jerusalem on an ass, as well as being similarly transported in the flight to Egypt, therefore provided an early symbolic association between Jesus and the fool/ass tradition. Even in triumphal entry into Jerusalem, Jesus came more as a fool's king than as a victorious hero. He rode not in a steed-drawn chariot of power and glory but on a lowly beast of burden, as if belonging to a mock procession among a conquered people. The early church was not long in making the further connection between the crucifixion of this Son of David and the suggestion of a cross on the donkey's back. Jesus was a fool's Messiah, a donkey-deliverer, a jester to the political and ecclesiastical kingdoms of earth.

Religious associations with the fool also moved in yet another direction in the holy-fool tradition, which appeared as early as the sixth century in the Greek Orthodox church and reached its fullest development in the Russian Orthodox church between the fourteenth and the seventeenth centuries.[10] A number of individuals were sainted as holy fools. Drawing upon the Pauline idea of the foolishness of Christian preaching, of the cross, and of God (1 Cor. 1:18–31), and of Christian disciples as "fools for Christ's sake [1 Cor. 4:10]," a type of sainthood developed in which the expression of piety was that of publicly making a fool of oneself. The monk or priest manifested his sincerity not by projecting an atmosphere of intense seriousness and sanctity, but by playing the part of the buffoon. He indicated his self-effacement by making himself ridiculous in his appearance and manner and thus becoming the object of mockery. He became, in effect, a jester to the church. Through a holy madness, feigned or real, analogous to that often found among court fools, he abased himself in a renunciation of spiritual pride and a revelation of the folly of the people. He humbled himself, as it were, in a comic identification with the humility and humiliation of Jesus—not the exalted Jesus of ecclesiastical pomp and pageantry, but the peasant Jesus who rode into Jerusalem on an ass as a scapegoat savior. Like the early Franciscans, who also called themselves "the world's fools" (*mundi moriones*), the holy fool withdrew from the riches and power and splendor of the church, as well as from elaborate scholastic theological disquisitions, to follow in the footsteps of a penniless itinerant who was hailed as king by being given mock robes and a crown of thorns and a cross for a throne.

The dangers of such associations with the fool tradition degenerating into outright sacrilege are evident in the many ecclesiastical attempts at suppression. And yet fools and their foolishness point to the necessity of permitting the periodic overturning of human hierarchies, of confounding human reason and its assured verities, of profaning the sacred altars of all earthly principalities and authorities. Such functions have, of course, been performed in all cultures, quite aside from comic figures and seasonal festivities, in the less formalized and more spontaneous indulgence in humor and nonsense. Whether in the repertoire of the "professional"—fool, jester, clown, humorist, comedian—or in the momentary remark of the "lay person," a perennial profusion of puns, anecdotes, and witticisms has always existed alongside sacred places, persons, beliefs, acts, and objects. They represent an inevitable, essential, and irrepressible human response to anything or anyone that is exalted to sacred status. Some are completely innocent, others quite risqué; some a profaning of holy things only in the sense of interspersing seriousness with humor, others more substantively in an overt caricature of religious concerns. Jokes and jests are constantly being evoked by those matters that we otherwise take with great seriousness, and all attempts at suppressing them are not only ineffectual but also misguided. It has been the characteristic concern of despots and dogmatists alike to safeguard dictates and doctrines from comic disturbances. Yet laughter at most is only driven underground.

Faith and Foolishness

It is most unfortunate that patristic and medieval Christianity did not include humor and humorlessness in its moral glossaries of the seven cardinal virtues and the seven deadly sins. Humility includes the ability to laugh at oneself and the refusal to take oneself seriously. Laughter may open the way to love and forgiveness, for in laughter hostilities are softened, just as forgiveness allows former enemies to laugh together. C. S. Lewis commented in the preface to his diabolical fantasy *The Screwtape Letters:*

Humor involves a sense of proportion and a power of seeing yourself from the outside. Whatever else we attribute to beings who sinned through pride, we must not attribute this. . . . We must picture Hell as a state where everyone is perpetually concerned about his own dignity and advancement, where everyone has a grievance, and where everyone lives the deadly serious passions of envy, self-importance and resentment.[11]

That little religious attention has been devoted to the relationship between the sacred and the comic, or faith and humor, is itself a reflection of the taboo mechanisms that commonly surround holy things. Laughter and humor, at first sight, seem quite out of place, and their object seems simply that of profaning the sacred or dissolving faith. Especially when the sacred is defined as the sphere of ultimate concerns and fundamental values, any introduction of the comic appears to be reducible to a failure to take sacred matters seriously, if not an outright rejection of their sacrality. The comic mood gives the initial impression of standing in contradiction both to the sacredness of the sacred and to the pious emotions and beliefs it should evoke. That which is sacred is only to be approached in fear and trembling, in aweful solemnity, in lowly obeisance and humble adoration, not in levity and gaiety. Humor, therefore, as Reinhold Niebuhr argued, is acceptable in the outer courts of the temple, and its echo may be heard in the sanctuary, but only faith, and not laughter, is appropriate in the Holy of Holies.[12] If there is "a time to laugh" and "a time to dance [Eccles. 3:4]" it is not around the altar but in the streets. And as the church has often insisted, there is a certain pagan aura that clings to fool's feasts, a sinful rebellion in profaning holy things, if not a bit of the rogue Satan in the devilish gleam in the eyes of the jester.

This type of attitude has been paid compliment by Harold Watts as "a by-product of that modesty which kept the comic writer strolling in the public square and which forbade him to have traffic with holy places, be they temples or churches, synagogues or chapels."[13] Yet something is missing in this view, apart from which faith is easy prey to fanaticism, sacred images and forms become idols, and salvation becomes spiritual bondage. The exclusion of humor from holy places might be a more plausible position if there were some universal agreement on what is and is not sacred. If only holy places somehow converged on a common Holy of Holies. But this is far from the case. It was, in fact, the sacrilization of everything from pebble to mountain and psyche to phallus—without any apparent common denominator suggestive of holiness—that led early theorists, such as Emile Durkheim and Sigmund Freud, to seek an understanding of the nature and power of the holy in sociological and psychological terms, rather than in religious terms. But insofar as religious faiths and holy places have served as bases of human unity, they have served just as successfully as bases of human disunity. Religion, which has elevated the human spirit with visions of common bonds, self-sacrifice, harmony, and compassion, has also proved to be one of the greatest single sources of segregation, pride, prejudice, antipathy, destruction, and bloodshed. Religious history is littered with reminders of the tragic possibilities of faith without humor and the sacred without the comic.

Religious expression at its best functions within a delicate dialectic between faith and laughter. On the one side is the peril of idolatry—the elevation of any finite form or understanding to an absolute, divine status. On the other side is the peril of a relativism for which nothing is sacred. Faith without laughter leads to dogmatism and self-righteousness. Laughter without faith leads to cynicism and despair. This is not to say what Reinhold Niebuhr has said—that humor represents a "no-man's-land" between faith and despair. There is a more intimate relationship between humor and faith than this. Humor does not stand midway between *faith* and despair but between *fideism* and despair, just as in the sociopolitical realm the jester stands midway between tyranny and anarchy. There is always the danger that humor without faith will fall into a cynicism concerning all meaning and value, where everything is doubted and nothing is holy any longer. But there is also the danger that faith without humor will fall into dogmatism and absolutism. Thus the melodramatic saviors of Gotham City, Batman and Robin, when in costume as the "Cape Crusaders," never cracked a smile, even in the midst of uttering the most pious banalities, while their adversaries—Joker, Penguin, Iceman, Catwoman, and company—never stopped laughing, and turned even crime into a parlor game.

If skepticism is the occupational hazard of fools and humorists, self-righteousness is the perennial temptation of prophets and priests. Whether formally acknowledged or not, this realization is intuitively sensed and irrepressibly expressed in a variety of informal ways in every age. As William Austin Smith observed in the iconography of Gothic architecture, "How one loves those laughing, indecorous imps one spies in Gothic cathedrals, safety valves of the comic perception of those bohemian journey-man builders, signaling to posterity their conviction that piety at high Gothic tension needs always the vigilant eye of the Comic Muse."[14]

The humorous remark or comic gesture is the footnote attached to every pious act and statement of belief that reminds us of our humanity, our mortality, our finiteness and fallibility, our foolishness. It is the parentheses placed around even our most serious and sacred moments which qualifies them as human moments, and the seriousness as human seriousness. To take oneself seriously *as a human being* is to laugh, for that which is taken in all sincerity and good faith as being ultimate is taken as such by human beings inhabiting this or that culture in this or that moment of time. Even the interpretation of faith as an ultimate and unconditional concern (e.g., Paul Tillich)[15] has an aura of ultimate and unconditional seriousness about it which human beings cannot give to their concerns without absolutizing their experiences and perceptions. Faith does not exclude humor any more than it excludes doubt, for faith is always being returned to the ultimate mysteries to which faith has responded and out of which faith has come.

Though the various forms of humor in relation to holy things may appear blasphemous, true blasphemy is to be found not in humor as such but in the *absence* of humor, for at the heart of the comic spirit and perspective is an acceptance of the prophetic warning against idolatry, and against that greatest blasphemy of all, the claim to understand or to be as God. Erasmus chided the scholastic theology of his time which, equipped with the most learned "definitions, arguments, corollaries, implicit and explicit propositions . . . abounding in newly-invented terms and prodigious vocables," undertook to divine the "most arcane matters, such as by what measure, and how long the perfect Christ was in the Virgin's womb, and how accidents subsist in the Eucharist without their subject," or whether an omnipotent God "could have taken upon Himself the likeness of a woman? Of a devil? Of an ass? Of a gourd?"[16]

The fool's function is humorously to profane the categories and hierarchies with which we would capture the ultimate truth about things, and add it as a human possession to the informational zoo of human knowledge. From the standpoint of the fool, who refuses to take any human pretensions or demarcations with absolute seriousness, the moat that defines and protects the king's castle is also the moat that imprisons the king. Hence, the neat patterns of rationality and value and order with which we organize and solidify our experience are confused and garbled by the fool. Sense is turned into nonsense, order into disarray, the unquestionable into the doubtful. The fool does not fit into, indeed refuses to fit into, the sacred conventions and hallowed structures of the human world. The fool is always about to bow the knee to earthly kingdoms, but never quite manages to go through with the motion. Instead, everything comes out wrong: the speech, the logic, the gestures, the decorum. Yet in this wrongness is a rightness of another sort. In this foolishness is another level of wisdom.

A common theme in the fool tradition is that all human beings are fools in their various ways, the stage fool and the social fool being only exemplars of a universal phenomenon. Moralistic fool literatures attempted to map out major types of human foolishness, but usually not in a way that included everyone. Fool rituals, however, were less discriminating. As the Mother of Folly answers in a sixteenth-century French farce, when asked who she is and where she comes from, "France, Flanders, Picardy, Normandy, England, Rome, Italy, Spain, Germany. I am at home in the courts of princes, among ecclesiastics and women, with students, beggars and lawyers. And I understand both astrology and theology."[17] In fact, rather than excluding religion or theology as representing some firm and unquestionable point of reference from which folly was to be seen and interpreted, the fool tradition has tended to take the position that all participate in a common folly (the comic equivalent of finitude and original sin). Within this common folly there is no higher folly than religious folly, precisely because religion claims to represent the highest authorities and to be dealing with the most ultimate questions of meaning and value.

A sixteenth-century comedy, *Des cris de Paris*, offered this description of "subtle fools":

They find such profundities in their minds
That if you were to believe their writings
You would think they were God's first cousins.[18]

Relative to the subtle fools, who are so confident in their genius and correctness of understanding, the fool tradition places the "simple fools," who readily believe anything anyone tells them, like the Yiddish "Gimpel" for whom everything was possible. When people would come to him and say, "Gimpel, there is a carnival in heaven," or "Gimpel, the rabbi has given birth to a calf" or "Gimpel, a cow flew over the roof and laid brass eggs," Gimpel believed them without question. If the subtle fool confuses faith with dogmatism and self-rightness, the simple fool confuses faith with credulity.

Like all comic figures, the fool is a reminder of the essential awkwardness of the human situation—an awkwardness that is only intensified in the religious situation. The awkwardness that is portrayed on a more trivial plane in the endless pratfalls of the clown, the predicaments of the comic hero, or the confusions of the fool reaches its climax in the religious situation as we attempt to deal with matters of ultimate concern and with the most fundamental questions of "reality." It is an awkwardness the comic side of which has never been adequately summarized in traditional philosophical or theological categories.

Take the case of the theologian whose office it is to articulate the implications of the faith and life of a particular religious community, the theologian who now, say, at the ripe age of thirty-five undertakes to give considered thought to the most encompassing issues of all, who ventures in fact systematically to explore the nature of God as God relates to the world, to develop a methodology appropriate to its divine object, perhaps even to engage in a respectable little "science of God." Whether acknowledged or not, the theologian is in the clumsiest of possible positions. The importance of the office notwithstanding, the very ultimacy of the object of inquiry makes of theology the highest form of foolishness.

The words of Yahweh to Job—who is in the midst of earnest reflection on the most tortuous of theological problems, having sought with fellow theologians over the space of thirty-seven chapters to interpret the relationship of the ways of God to the fortunes of humankind—well express the humorousness as well as the pathos of the religious situation: "Where were you when I laid the foundation of the earth [Job 38:4]?" It is as if a celebrated theologian of the church had just completed the final declarations of a one-, two-, three-, or perhaps twelve-volume systematic on "nature, man and God," expecting to hear the words "Well done, thou good and faithful servant," only to hear instead, "Where were you when I laid the foundation of the earth?"

Karl Barth, in his twelve-volume (and at that unfinished) *Church Dogmatics*, gave a scant two pages to humor—and in doing so exceeded the attentions of most theologians. Nevertheless, in his later years he remarked concerning these prodigious theological efforts,

The angels laugh at old Karl. They laugh at him because he tries to grasp the truth about God in a book of Dogmatics. They laugh at the fact that volume follows volume and each is thicker than the previous ones. As they laugh, they say to one another, "Look! Here he comes now with his little pushcart full of volumes of the *Dogmatics!*"[19]

In this manner the great corpus of his theological investigations is finally placed within the parentheses of the comic perspective in a simple confession of the humanity of all theology.

Humor carries us beyond all our theisms, and our atheisms as well, for humor corresponds to both the awkwardness of religious inquiry and the inexhaustible mystery of the object of that inquiry. Every Holy of Holies points ultimately to the Mystery of Mysteries. In Gerardus van der Leeuw's words,

The religious significance of things . . . is that one which no wider or deeper meaning can follow. It is the meaning of the whole; it is the last word. But this meaning is never understood, this last word is never spoken; always they remain superior, the ultimate meaning being a secret which reveals itself repeatedly, only nevertheless to remain eternally concealed. It implies an advance to the farthest boundary, where only one sole fact is understood: that all comprehension is "beyond."[20]

Before this Mystery all participate in a common foolishness. And the subtle fool may be no closer to the truth of things than the simple fool.

Chapter 3

Putting Humpty-Dumpty Together Again

Here is a man like himself, only more pathetic and miserable, with ludicrously impossible clothes—in every sense a social misfit and failure. . . . [Yet] he has a protective air of mock dignity, takes the most outrageous liberties with people, and wears adversity as though it was a bouquet.

—Charles Chaplin[1]

Clowns require no announcement or introduction. When they appear they are immediately recognizable by everyone, regardless of their location, costuming, or behavior. Whether bursting in upon a tribal ritual, ancient comedy, festival parade, circus ring, or modern cinema, their presence is unmistakable. There are clowns who are silent and clowns who are subtle, but there are no incognito clowns. Clowns refuse to be missed or ignored.

The clown suddenly materializes within the workaday world or the sacred arena like some imagined visitor from outer space, a roaring monster from a funhouse grotto come to life in graceful, jerky motion, a brightly colored child's toy wound up for a noisy moment. At times the clown seems like some harmless escapee from an asylum for the insane, come to sweep away neatness and stir up the settled dust of our lives. At other times the clown resembles a ghostly apparition from the spirit world, paradoxically seeking with grinning death-mask to renew life and revive our slumping spirits.

Yet despite their antiquity and their clamorous familiarity, clowns present an enigmatic image. They offer such a jumble of identities and loose ends as to prevent simple definition. From Indian rituals to modern circuses, they stand there with great ringed eyes and mouths upon gaily painted faces, outlandish in gesture and attire, perhaps with wild hair or a bald spot or a little of both, grinning and leapfrogging about in defiance of easy description and common understanding—and defying a great many other things as well. One may bounce along like a polka-dotted balloon, while another strides about like a long stick on stilts. There may be a friendly giant out of a child's fairyland, or a mischievous dwarf from a leprechaun legend. Clowns are, as a Navaho term for them translates, "delight-makers" (*Koshare*). But they are also, as the police officers in many a Chaplin or Keaton film would have phrased it, "disturbers of the peace." And while they seem to epitomize the grossness and density of matter and flesh, they persist in floating around in a freedom of spirit that is at least six inches off the ground. The plane of their being seems to intersect some other dimension of space and time.

Clowns are so childlike, yet so adult; so human, yet so nonhuman; so vivid, yet so unreal; so oversexed, yet so asexual; so bold, yet so easily scared away. They can be devilishly knowing in their winks, yet bear such an innocent look on their faces. They are permitted considerable license in their behavior, but not without being chased and punished for their offenses. At their best they are hilarious, but with a touch of sadness and perhaps wearing a tear or a frown. Clowns move somewhere between order and disorder, life and death, hope and despair. To the very small child, especially up close and all-of-a-sudden, they are often ugly and frightening, like ogres with a grotesquely terrifying presence. But they are actually both ugly and beautiful, terrible and funny. And their relationship to society is equally ambiguous, as among the Yaqui Indians, where clowns both profane Holy Week and its liturgies and act as police officers who restrain others from getting out of line.[2]

The High Priest of Fun and Laughter

While it is impossible, therefore, to give any simple definition to the clown, one element is always there. And through that element the disparate pieces of our existence are joined in a kind of madcap shotgun wedding. The clown is laughter incarnate: the "prophet, priest, and king" of laughter. After all, one of the purposes of the clown is to have fun and be funny. But the clown is not fun and funny only in a momentary and miscellaneous manner in which we laugh and have done with it. The laughter elicited is not just a random tickle on the periphery of our existence. The laughter is not just a random tickle on the periphery of our existence. The clown is funny in a profound and provocative manner. We are touched at the center of our existence. The clown dares to sport in the inner sanctum of our being, for this is the joke about *ourselves*, suddenly realized. The clown is the multiplicity without us and within us openly and humorously displayed—the whole range of conflicting human emotions and aspirations clapped together in one great ovation of applause.

The clown is the personification of much else besides laughter, sometimes even of pathos and sorrow and death. But the center of gravity is in laughter, and all those other uniquely human capacities that are associated with a comic sensibility and that separate us from both animals and computers. If we are "laughing animals" (*homo risens*), with the peculiar ability to play with our existence, to imagine other possibilities and impossibilities too, to take words and things and circumstances in multiple senses, to stand back and joke about anything and everything—then the clown is zany proof that we are human and not monkeys or machines.

Even in the form of the poker-faced Keaton who never smiled, or the sad-faced Emmett Kelly who had little to smile about, clowns are laughable and lovable. They are still the agents of laughter, officiants in a special ritual of mirth and foolishness. They are knights without armor come to battle without swords and disarm us all. When Kelly the ragged bum is incapable of performing the simplest of tasks—like sweeping the floor—correctly and without mishap, or when a deft Buster Keaton stares in blank resignation at the collapsed house to which he has just given a final hammerblow, we laugh. We are called to laughter. And we laugh not only because analogous misfortunes have happened to us, leaving us feeling similarly inadequate and helpless, but also because we are capable of taking even the darkest and most painful situations in more than one way. We are not limited to one-possibility responses. We are not eternally confined to taking things straight and univocally. In laughter we transcend not only the animals but also ourselves and our circumstances. We transcend disappointment and suffering. We transcend the jumbled contradictions of our lives. We transcend even the self-imposed requirement that life always make sense, conform to a plan, work out, give us our due, or be equitable and just.

The best modern example of these comic capacities is still Chaplin's tramp figure. Chaplin as a child had known what it meant to be poor and a nobody. He had known what it meant to wear cast-off and mismatched clothing, to eat cheap herbs and stale bread and doubtful eggs, to walk slum streets and live in one room, to have creditors come to carry off whatever few possessions one had, to be taken to workhouses and orphanages. And he never forgot this in his films. Most of his films started out from the remembrance of what it meant to be hungry and cold and jobless and penniless and alone. Charlie was never the clown who simply enters the arena in the midst of festivity and gala celebration to bring laughter to tables that are already sumptuously laden with holiday feasts, and everyone is already singing and dancing in their finest attire. Charlie entered the world of his films in the lowest and darkest hour, where there was poverty and suffering, where despair was easy and hope was hard and joy almost impossible. The little tramp came like a character out of the London slums of Dickens's *Oliver Twist* or *A Christmas Carol*, yet miraculously transformed into a figure that was as comic as it was pathetic.

In *City Lights*, Charlie is homeless and jobless, sleeping where he can. In *Life* he is in a flophouse. In *Police* he is an exconvict with nowhere to go. In *The Vagabond* he is a vagabond. In *The Circus* he is left alone in an empty, littered field when the circus has moved on. In *The Kid* he rescues a boy being taken away to an orphanage, and he eludes the law with an orphan girl in *Modern Times*. In *The Gold Rush* he is so hungry that he boils his leather shoe for dinner. In *The Champion* he shares his last sausage with a bulldog.

But in the midst of all this misery and deprivation the little clown came, with his antics and his human tenderness and his magical transformations. He came with a plucky spirit that refused to be dismissed or ignored or overcome. He came with a sense of individual worth and personal pride for the lowliest of the low—for who could be lower than Charlie? He came with a measure of hope that might give in to tears but would not give in to despair. He didn't stop to philosophize. He didn't stand there waiting for Godot. He didn't stand there waiting for anybody. And we saw in him what stout and resilient people we were or could be. As Chaplin said of the Charlie he had created,

I am always aware that Charlie is playing with Death. He plays with it, mocks it, thumbs his nose at it, but it's always there. He is aware of death at every moment of his existence, and he is terribly aware of being alive. . . . And he is bringing more life. That is his only excuse, his only purpose.[3]

This meaning of the clown is not peculiar to the modern West. In the mythological recounting of the history of the Jemez Indians, for example, it is this role as agent of transcendence that is credited to the clown. When the Jemez emerged from a hole in the earth to the far north, they found food to be scarce and the weather inhospitable. So they began a long, arduous journey to the south. As they migrated they had difficulty finding food along the way, their blankets wore out, and many died of cold and hunger. The survivors attempted to be courageous, but as their numbers were continuously being depleted, they too prayed to die—whereupon the Moon Mother entreated the Sun Father to come to the aid of the Jemez. So the Sun Father created the clown.

The Sun took one of the survivors of our people, painted his body in transverse black and white bands, decorated his hair with corn husks, and suspended eagle feathers behind each ear. As soon as he was thus painted and decorated, this man became a "funny man," and began to dance, cut capers, and make grimaces. So interested did the people become in his performing that they forgot their sorrows and became glad. They then resumed their journey . . . which they continued till they reached the Rio Grande.[4]

It is interesting that the Sun Father does not rescue the Jemez from the problems of cold and hunger and death, but rather provides a vehicle for coping with these hardships and misfortunes that are a normal part of life. It is also interesting that the "funny man" enters not at the point where there is health and plenty to celebrate but at the lowest and darkest hour. He invites laughter and gladness, despite the fact that there is little to celebrate. He is the renewer of courage and hope and the will to live.

The myth-teller continues by recounting how, when the Jemez reached the warm lands of the south, they were attacked by other tribes who drove them into caves. But they kept their spirit, and a hero was sent who dispelled the enemies of the Jemez and taught them how to build villages, hunt, and perform the proper religious rites. "And he made the clown-dancers [*Koshare*] the sprouters of grain (the spring-summer clowns). He made the funny men [*Kurena*] the maturers of grain and of everything that lives and grows upon the earth (the fall-winter clowns)." The hero also gave them the power to represent the people before the gods.

Similarly, among the Laguna and Kere Pueblos, the Corn Mother is said to have wished to have someone to make her laugh and to make people laugh. So she rubbed her skin and rolled a piece of her skin into a ball, covering it with a blanket. From underneath the blanket came the clown (*Koshare*) "to make fun, and to make people forget their troubles." The Corn Mother then created the rainbow for the clown to climb up and down on.[5]

The Pueblo clown, as the high priest of fun and laughter, is given a rainbow as a ladder, and the power to represent others before the gods. With this rainbow, and the clown's own "rainbowishness," the clown restores color to life, combines the various hues of our being, and offers a sign of hope. While there is no promise of a pot of gold at the end of the rainbow, nor any guarantee against future hardship or catastrophe, this clown does point to a means of bringing light out of human mud and limitation. And we are enabled to laugh once more.

The Catholicity of the Clown

The Pueblo clown displays another common trait of clowning—that of being a mediator, a go-between, a *doppelganger* as the Germans put it. The mediation takes place by means of the clown's own special form of the *axis mundi*—the sacred pole at the center of the world—the rainbow ladder. The clown climbs up and down, brightly and garishly, between sky and earth, the divine and the human, the human and the animal, one person and another, and the various zones of our individual being. No one plane or zone can define or hold the clown, who moves, leaps, slips and stumbles back and forth among them all. Through the rainbow ladder and the clown's own coat of many colors are reconnected the many fragmented shades of our existence, if only by tossing them laughingly side-by-side and calling their ephemeral combination a link between the heavens and the earth.

One reason clowning is so difficult to define is that clowns take upon themselves the human diversity, encompassing in their grab-bag generosity the most varied examples of the species and its behavior. In so doing, clowns also encompass those areas of tension and conflict within a given society or within human nature as such. If clowns were given to reciting nursery rhymes, the favorite would likely be "Humpty-Dumpty."

Humpty-Dumpty sat on a wall;
Humpty-Dumpty had a great fall;
And all the king's horses and all the king's men
Couldn't put Humpty-Dumpty together again.

This is a clown's view of human existence, and the sort of predicament with which clowning is often dealing. In this kaleidoscopic identity the clown is many people and many moods, formed and reformed out of the same disparate pieces of humanity. Thus clowns come in all sizes and shapes, in all colors and wrappings. They may be tall or short, thin or fat, with a coat of many colors or covered with mud and feathers. The European harlequin was as brilliant as a peacock, while among the Jicarilla Apache the clown was known as "striped excrement." Clowns dramatize the fragmented and alienated character of our individual and social existence, yet at the same time offer a kind of resolution of it. They propose to do what "all the king's horses and all the king's men" couldn't do: put the Humpty-Dumpty of our humanity back together again.

Basically there are two ways in which this ritual brokenness and reunion is carried out in clowning. One is by means of a comic duo that embraces certain extremes of the human spectrum. Oliver Hardy was plump and domineering; Stan Laurel was skinny and browbeaten. Harpo Marx never spoke a word; Groucho Marx never stopped talking. Mae West was the seductively aloof beauty cooing, "Come on up and see me some time"; W. C. Fields was the puffed and puffing scalawag who had difficulty climbing the stairs. Dean Martin was the handsome, urbane, crooning ladies' man; Jerry Lewis was the awkward, bungling, daffy, squeaky-voiced kid that only a stray mutt could love.

Among the Pueblo, clowning involved a marked contrast between the restrained bearing and colorful striping of the *Koshare*, and the grossness of the *Koyemshi* smeared with mud, and the *Ne'wekwe* who drank urine.[6] In the European circus and stage, clowns have often appeared in the antithetical forms of the elegant white-face and the shabby Augusto. The white-face clown performs acts of skill and grace, uses plain white makeup with accented beauty lines, wears splendid hats and costuming and shoes, and parades with the poise and comeliness of a fashion model. The Augusto, by contrast, uses bizarre makeup, displays jarring colors and lines, and wears tattered and mismatched clothes, funny hats, and outrageous shoes. The Augusto is anything but august: a dunce, a bungler, a mess, a disaster area.

In this manner, two opposite kinds of comic figures are set in dialectical motion. Our whole being is put joltingly together by the simple device of slapping opposites against one another. The other, more complex and ambitious type is the solo clown, who manages to contain such polarities within a single figure. From tribal to circus clowning, one finds figures who in their body-paint or costuming stripe themselves black and white or yellow and green, or wear a ragtag jumble of colors. If they wear oversized shoes, they will like as not wear an undersized hat. If they give themselves a gaudy smile, they will probably also add a tear. If they are graceful one moment, they will likely be jerky the next. They may tiptoe like a ballerina on a case of eggs, then race through a vegetable market like a crazed bull. They will walk ever so carefully, then trip most clumsily. Or they will take precisely measured aim with a large wooden hammer and then smash the thumb carelessly left holding the peg. In this form the clown is the bearer of Walt Whitman's self-affirmation:

Do I contradict myself? Very well,
I contradict myself; I am large,
I contain multitudes.[7]

Buster Keaton capitalized on an expressionless and seemingly inert "stone face" in contrast to great agility and an almost frantic movement of the body. He could run, dart, climb, catapult, leap, and paddle himself out of the most inescapable dangers! Yet to the many kinds of crises in which he found himself, Keaton turned the same immovable stare. Face and body, and face and situation, seemed to have nothing to do with each other, as if belonging to separate stories. Even those circumstances that might normally precipitate intense emotional expression—fear, anger, hatred, dismay, elation, passion, laughter—were taken with a passivity that would be the envy of both gods and Zen masters. The human extremes of serenity and frenzy, aloofness and involvement, innocence and knowledgeability, were hilariously united like clashing cymbals.

Claude Levi-Strauss developed the thesis—previously applied by Hegel to tragedy—that the function of myth is that of reconciling points of conflict and tension within a given human context. The logic of myth is that of mediating contraries. Thus, the oppositions between life and death, fertility and killing, agriculture and hunting, may be mythically represented by herbivorous and carnivorous animals that are reconciled in the narrative by the figure of an omnivorous animal.[8] The clown in these terms shares in the same mythic functions. The clown as "Everyman" is the representative of the many-sidedness of our existence and the tensions between sides—not any one side or set of characteristics. The clown is omnivorously human.

Chaplin was the most successful in this role of any of the early film clowns, and perhaps in the whole history of clowning. It started with the playful donning of Fatty Arbuckle's ample trousers and Chester Conklin's tight-fitting coat. To this were added shoes too large and a hat too small and a flexible cane that was itself a functional contradiction. Then Chaplin added the laborious, shuffling, penguin-walk of an old cabdriver he had seen hobbling along in London to what was otherwise a youthful, light-footed, acrobatic figure. The paradoxes that such combinations produced and made possible were so many and so profound that even to Chaplin the resulting figure was a mysterious being that seemed to have been revealed to him and that he would have to spend much of the rest of his career exploring. He said later, "For me he was fixed, complete, the moment I looked in the mirror and saw him for the first time; yet even now I don't know all the things there are to be known about him."[9]

Chaplin knew very well, however, the extremes that were surfacing out of his own experience and uniting themselves in the unusual form of Charlie. He was beginning to earn good money at the same time, and he was soon to become the highest-paid actor in the world. But he had come from a broken home in one of the poorest sections of London, his father dying in an alcoholic ward, his mother taken to a mental institution, and young Charles put in an orphanage. In Charlie the clown, Chaplin was putting himself and his world together. The elements were partly happenstance. But he had taken, in effect, the fastidious bowler hat, dress coat, white shirt, black tie, and walking stick of an English gentleman and combined them with the baggy pants, floppy shoes, and unkemptness of the poor and the homeless. The top and the bottom of the social order were thus thrown together in one person. The oppositions between rich and poor were simultaneously intensified and softened. Chaplin was henceforth *both* gentleman and tramp, and *neither* gentleman nor tramp. The most extreme ends of the social spectrum were contained, united, and transcended in one slender individual. Chaplin recalled his first interpretation of the clown character to Mack Sennett in 1914:

This fellow is manysided, a tramp, a gentleman, a poet, a dreamer, a lonely fellow, always hopeful of romance and adventure. He would have you believe he is a scientist, a musician, a duke, a polo player. However, he is not above picking up cigarette butts or robbing a baby of its candy.[10]

Human beings, after all, from lofty to lowly are both meticulous and sloppy, polite and crude, graceful and awkward, rational and irrational. The aristocrat in fine clothes and suave sophistication was revealed as being something of a bum underneath. And the bum, despite a crumpled appearance and bad manners, was revealed as having a certain dignity and grace. Charlie as an aristocrat and Charlie as a bum were equally delightful and equally ludicrous and equally incomplete. And in their union was affirmed a common humanity that lay beneath all those distinctions and separations to which we ordinarily grant such importance.

Given this paradoxical being, Chaplin would often play in sudden turn the gentleman and the hobo, the bully and the coward, the tyrant and the impotent, the tenderhearted sentimentalist and the devilish little trickster. In *Life*, Chaplin, finding himself in a flophouse, puts fellow tramps to sleep in the most direct manner by striking them on the head with a wooden mallet, then dutifully and motheringly kissing them goodnight. Or he carefully disposes of his cigar ash in the open mouth of a snoring drunk, in preparation for kneeling beside his cot to pray. In *Easy Street* he good-heartedly aids in the distribution of food to children in a local orphanage, but he does so as if he were scattering birdseed to pigeons. In *The Tramp* he thoughtfully helps another farmhand off with his boots, but when one boot does not slip off easily he kicks him in the face to dislodge it. Or he "helps" his partner carry feed sacks by prodding him in the rear end with a pitchfork as if it were a cattle prod.

In these terms Chaplin approximated the total clown in a way in which few clowns have ever succeeded. This, no doubt, is one reason he had such universal and enduring appeal. He was nobody in particular, yet everybody all at once. No one could stand outside the parentheses of his bowler hat and floppy shoes. He was, as Robert Payne said, "the whole human comedy wrapped in a single frail envelope of flesh."

Aristotle defined the ludicrous as a species of the ugly, and the comic figure as one who portrayed inferior people. But this definition misses the extent to which comic characters can be both inferior and superior, ugly and beautiful, simultaneously. Chaplin as the tramp had the beauty and grace of the white-faced clown, yet all the awkward and slovenly character of the Augusto. There was certainly a handsome, polished, lovable side to Charlie, no matter how disheveled and dirty and uncouth the little tramp might be. But, unlike the mighty hero or the film idol, his was not an unblemished beauty or dashing heroism. He could order people about and stand proudly with an air of complete mastery and assurance. He could become terribly self-important, as occasion might permit. Yet in a twinkling he could become equally subservient and cowering. Now and then he would make some heroic attempt at saving maidens in distress, but defending maidens was usually mixed with hiding behind them. His heroism involved a strong aversion to pain and a distinct preference for running. It was always abundantly clear that he participated in the total human condition.

In his trampishness, Charlie was very close to the level of sheer animal survival much of the time, where elegance is irrelevant and where one easily disposes of most of the niceties and pleasantries of "polite society." Yet even as a tramp, and therefore at the bottom of the bottom of the human kingdom, he restored a sense of worth and pride to the lowliest, most forlorn individual. In his very tatters and tumbles he was still endearing and still very human.

The genius of Chaplin was that in the figure of the tramp he embraced a common humanness. He expressed what we all are: both beauty and beast, domesticated and uncivilized, clothed and naked. In biblical terms he was both the noble creature of Genesis 1, created in the image and likeness of God, and the clay figurine of Genesis 2, fashioned from the dust of the earth, and with a considerable dustiness clinging to him. As the tramp he was clearly enough close to the earth most of the time. But if he was down, he was never out. He had style and deftness and bravado, and an unconquerable sense of his own importance. Yet if he put on too many airs, as circumstances might permit, he was quickly dumped back in the dirt again—if he did not suddenly leap there himself.

In an episode in *City Lights*, Charlie is driving a Rolls-Royce convertible that belongs to a rich man who has befriended him. For a moment Charlie's trampishness gives way to the opposite, which is already prefigured in his top hat, coattails, vest, and cane: aristocratic snobbishness. He drives the Rolls around the city streets with his head cocked back in an air of superiority and self-importance and with all the dignity of a gentleman—or at least the *chauffeur* of a gentleman. But as he turns a corner, he spies a cigar butt on the sidewalk. He spies it in fact at the same time that another tramp, busily patrolling the gutters, has spotted it. Charlie's *other self* makes no hesitation in returning. He brings the Rolls to an abrupt stop, leaps out, and just as the gutterbum is leaning over to pick up the cigar butt, Charlie kicks him aside, grabs the prize, jumps back into the limousine, and speeds off—to the utter astonishment and bewilderment of the hapless bum.

The clown insists on putting side-by-side many of those things that we spend considerable time keeping in separate pockets or separate rooms or separate drawers of the mind: altruism and selfishness, rationality and impulse, religion and sex, kings and commoners, Rolls-Royces and cigar butts. The clown identifies our tensions and our ambivalences, running and leaping to and from "the other side of the tracks." Then suddenly we find ourselves put back together again in a hilarious slam-bang fashion. And this is the clown's peculiar form of salvation: a comic ritual of redemption for the human race.

The Lord of Ambiguity

What we are reluctant to acknowledge, but what the clown fixes on, is that we are composed of and dream of contraries. We fantasize about complete freedom and complete security, rugged individualism and social harmony, amorous adventures and marital bliss, higher wages and lower prices, something worth fighting for . . . and peace and tranquillity. We project utopias where material goods abound cheaply and plentifully for all, and Edenic gardens free of trash and litter and tourists and nuclear dumping grounds. We imagine a world in which things are imperishable and a world in which everything is easily discarded and biodegradable, so we develop indestructible plastics and disposable diapers.

"Self-contradiction," as Wolfgang Zucker has argued, "is the clown's most significant feature. Whatever predicate we use to describe him, the opposite can also be said, and with equal right."[11] Yet the self-contradictions and incongruities that the clown incarnates are held together in a single, mysteriously particularized human being. The clown seems schizophrenic and clearly displays our individual and collective schizophrenias, yet without coming completely unglued or flying apart at the seams. The clown seems awkwardly unified at the same time—like the awkwardnesses of sexual union—which is one reason the awkwardness can be so funny. What we all are is expressed to some degree or other, but in a way that does not leave us torn and broken. In this odd figure the complexities of our being and the cross-purposes of our lives are patched and pinned loosely and playfully together. We are judged and accepted, humbled and healed, divided and united—all in the same comic ritual.

The clown has commonly been referred to, along with the fool, as the "lord of disorder" and "lord of misrule," and suspected of having some sort of unholy alliance with the devil. True, the Greek god Momus, lord of pleasantry and patron of clowns (mummers), was the son of Nox (noxious) and grandson of Chaos, while Discord, Death, and the Furies were his brethren. And certainly the clown introduces a large element of chaos and confusion into every situation and has a special talent for profaning holy things. But this is hardly the full sum of the function involved.

The key to the paradox of the clown's person and performance is a disturbing yet liberating ambiguity. The clown is now this and now that, and neither this nor that. Whether the relationship is to order or disorder, rationality or irrationality, sacred or profane, that relationship is ambiguous. Ordinary canons of dress and decorum do not apply. Colors and accessories, sizes and styles, sense and nonsense are mixed together in the most mad and marvelous manner. The rules of etiquette or social distinction or sexual propriety are not carefully followed or kept. Like John Gardner's Sunshine Man,[12] the clown does not subscribe to the laws of the state or of reason—and sometimes not even to the laws of gravity.

But this does not mean that clowning is simply anarchic or antisocial, or cynical with respect to reason and truth. Clowns are not "simply" anything. Thus no specific sacred or moral order can contain them. No social rule or standard can measure them. No logical or aesthetic category can exhaust them. Whatever the understanding of the holy or definition of truth, beauty, and goodness, they do not fit. They are blurred and relativized. The clown breaks through all the boxes and badges with which we package and label our lives or attempt to confine others.

In *The Pilgrim*, for example, Chaplin played the dual role of an escaped convict who had disguised himself in the only available clothing on hand at the time: the garb of a clergyman. The two social poles of convict and minister are thus suddenly united in a single person who now becomes, quite ambiguously, both. In his flight from the law, Charlie takes a train out West. But when he alights from the train in a small southwestern frontier town, he is mistaken for the eagerly awaited pastor of the local church. Charlie makes a valiant effort at preaching and otherwise playing the role. He recalls some Bible stories from his youth and renders them in the style of a theatrical evangelist. But he has certain bad habits that betray another identity. During the morning offering he has nothing to do, so he sits down, crosses his legs, and lights up a cigarette!

Once the convict/minister double identity is discovered, we are introduced to the larger ambiguities of law and lawlessness. Rather than face a return to prison, Charlie is mercifully escorted by the town sheriff to the Mexican border to freedom/exile. Yet no sooner does he cross the border than he finds himself in the middle of a shoot-out between Mexican bandits. The film ends with Charlie running along the border, hopping back and forth from one side to the other, then waddling off with one foot in Mexican "lawlessness" and one foot in American "law and order," trying his best to mediate between the two and comically transcending them both.

The clown is not the lord of disorder per se. A more appropriate designation would be the lord of ambiguity and relativity. The clown is lord of that no-man's-land between contending forces, moving back and forth along all those human lines drawn (not without arbitrariness) between law and order, social and antisocial, reason and irrationality, friend and foe, fashionable and unfashionable, important and unimportant. The clown is now on one side, now on the other, and ultimately both and neither. And one of the ritual functions of clowning is to convey a sense of this ambiguity and of the relativity that clings to all finite categories.

Clowns thus often look like mottled figments of our dreams, hovering between nightmares and visions of sugarplums. They are so many pieces of fantasy and reality sewn haphazardly together and precariously held in place by strings and pins and suspenders—as all of us are, even in our relative normality. They are the multiplicity of human emotions and tendencies, broken apart and reassembled in a surprising and sometimes shocking manner.

Dreams are what clowns are made of, as much as dreams are what myths are made of. There are good dreams and bad dreams, glimpses of greatness and realizations of weakness; hopes and fears; recollections of childhood and anticipations of old age; the dance of life and the dance of death; joy and sadness. And the unreal reality of dreams is there too in a strange assortment of shapes and colors and movements. The clown comes to us as a denizen of this world of myth and dream where rationality and irrationality are mixed, a flood of apparently disconnected images thrown up from the subconscious and united in surrealistic combinations.

The curious result of all this is not, as one might expect, a dark and disconcerting awareness of the labyrinthine tangle of human life. One is not left with the sinking feeling that the way has been lost, a light has failed, or former verities have been called into question. Life does not seem suddenly dislocated or disoriented. The result, in fact, is a renewed sense of freedom, a liberation of the spirit. One finds new faith in the elasticity of the species, a larger vision of humanity, a more inclusive acceptance of the manyness of the self and other selves. And the world does not seem as inflexible and confining as it had been before, if only because someone has taken a smoke during the morning offering.

The Koyemshi (Mudhead) clowns of the Hopi and Zuni tribes find mythological justification for their ambiguous roles by tracing their ancestry to the twelve Koyemshi born of an incestuous relationship between a primal brother and sister. The twelve offspring are said to have been afflicted with one or another of the twelve human imperfections: gloominess, cowardice, fear, ugliness, pride, and so on. The Koyemshi clowns, therefore, take upon themselves the imperfections of the people and offer themselves as objects of laughter. Yet they are privy to a special knowledge and power. "Silly were they, yet wise as the gods and high priests . . . the oracles of all olden sayings and deep meanings."[13]

The scatological practices among some of the clown societies of the Pueblo Indians, particularly the Zuni, are notorious examples of this clownish capacity for pointing to and containing the total human condition. One is initiated into the Zuni Ne'wekwe order by a ritual of filth-eating—a strange sort of eucharist indeed. Mud and excrement are smeared on the body for the clown performance, and major and minor parts of the performance may consist of sporting with excreta, smearing and daubing it, or drinking urine and pouring it on one another. Among the Hopi, a group of males known as "singers" play about with vulva-shaped sticks during initiation ceremonies, singing taunting and obscene songs to the women and running after them to "bless them" with filth. The women, in turn, being well-prepared, douse the singers with foul water or urine.[14]

This may not be one of the more palatable aspects of clown symbolism. And relative to it, more "civilized" clowning may seem tame. Yet it is there, and in some historic contexts very much there—just as it is universally present in all societies in coarse language, jokes, and pranks. The clown, through comical associations with these aspects of our existence, returns us to the preformal, and to the dust from which we have emerged to breathe the breath of life. This is not only a comedown from the more splendid images we have of ourselves, but also a reaffirmation of the total human condition. Our muddiness is not to be dismissed as impure and profane and shameful. It is fundamentally good.

The clown reduces life to its basics. Hence the common association of clowning with food, sex, and evacuation in exaggerated proportions (gluttony, obscenity, and scatological play). For all our pious creeds and momentous concerns, the basic requirements of our lives are relatively simple: a good meal and restful sleep, freedom from anxiety and freedom from constipation, the enjoyment of sex and the laughter of children, the satisfaction of work and the pleasure of play, the conviviality of friends and a moment's peace. Among the natural contexts for clowning, therefore, have always been the carnival season and the springtime and harvest rituals, where the *joi de vivre* is paramount and the renewal of life through food and fertility is celebrated. Without life, after all, there is no reason, no morality, no religion. And without fertility and food and the elimination of bodily wastes, there is no life. Life and the sources of life are primary. We cannot live by spirit alone.

Thus the Koyemshi clown of the Zuni and Hopi Indians comes forth with body smeared with the red-brown mud from around the sacred springs of the tribe, as did the first Koyemshi. He is mud and spirit combined. If he profanes sacred matters, he comes from the sacred springs themselves. If he disrupts the Kachina dancers, he combines the primordial powers of earth and water which make possible the dance. He wears the six primary colors, which represent the four directions, the zenith and the nadir of Pueblo cosmology. He is a comic/cosmic symbol of the total context of life. And he encompasses the whole of the human microcosm as well—in William Lynch's words—"down to the last inch of the little beastie."

The clown is more than an iconoclast or a satirist. There is more here than an invasion of sacred precincts or a puncturing of high-flying balloons or a kicking of pompous asses. There is also an element of celebration of this common humanity of ours, a fundamental yea-saying to the curious business of being mortal creatures of the earth. Being "all too human" is not seen as necessarily a great weight that drags us down or a curse that has been placed upon us, but something potentially delightful, as clowns are delightful. For the proud and pretentious this may not be so delightful, or for those who require clean lines, precise calculations, absolute points of reference, and clear and distinct ideas, clownish revelations may not be so amusing. But for those who are not pretenders to thrones that are not theirs or to a divinity they have not attained, or even to some superior form of humanity, the clown enables us to embrace ourselves and one another as the luminous lumps that we are.

In the form of the clown we feel, as Nathan Scott once wrote of Charlie the tramp, "that here is the real human thing itself—clothed not in the unearthly magnificence of tragic heroism, but in the awkward innocence of an essential humanity."15

The Child

Chapter 4

A Fool's Liturgy

Give me such philosophic thoughts
that I can rejoice everywhere I go
In the lovable oddity of things.
—Carmen B. de Gasztold
"The Prayer of the Elephant"[1]

The clown wishes to buy a ring for his lady. He is handed a precious jewel. He examines it, shrugs his shoulders, turns up his nose, and tosses it in the dirt like a common pebble. Then he reaches into the dirt and picks up a common pebble, which he proceeds to admire as if it were a precious jewel. And in some larger sense it really is a precious jewel, except that our ordinary canons of value have taught us to prize certain stones, pay large sums for them, and use them to measure status and wealth—while at the same time we disparage pebbles, ignore them, and in like manner flatten out vast regions of our experience which suffer by comparison with those few things to which we restrict our attentions and treasurings.

Harvey Cox in his *Feast of Fools* has argued that the appropriateness of the clown as a religious symbol is as the "personification of festivity and fantasy." And Cox has identified as the essential ingredients of this feast of fools "conscious excess," "celebrative affirmation," and "juxtaposition" (i.e., that which is "noticeably different from everyday life").[2] While this is partially correct, it does not necessarily direct us to the right fools or the whole "feast." In fact, one of the peculiarities of a

73

fool's feast is that by the usual standards it often appears to be no feast at all, but rather a feast *for* fools. We are escorted, as it were, into an elegant dining hall gaily decorated for merrymaking, only to discover that beneath the lid of the silver serving platter are the crisp remains of a common sparrow!

Though clowns in their frivolity and garish attire are certainly party to, and even officiants in, festivity and fantasy, one must be careful to note the unusual character of their revelry. Clowns, after all, are most ambiguous figures. They may appear to be from another planet, but they are authentically this-worldly. Not only do they stand outside and over against the sphere of ordinary existence, merrily transporting their audience into some Land of Enchantment, but they also revalue life by standing, at the same time, most deeply and humanly within it. Clowns move between fantasy and reality, the sublime and the commonplace. That is a part of their mediation, their dialectic, their salvation.

The Celebration of the Commonplace

The world of the clown is not just a secondary world of fantasy that soars away from our world on balloons and kite strings and butterfly dreams. And it is not always "noticeably different from everyday life." In many respects it is noticeably *like* everyday life. The props and tricks of clowning are usually nothing spectacular at all. The clown will pull from baggy trousers a lollipop or a string of sausages, perhaps a paper geranium or a whistle, and act as though it were wonderful to do so. Though there is a suggestion of eating sumptuously, the actual diet is likely to consist of long chains of hot dogs and great bunches of bananas. In costuming and accoutrement, the clown often appears to have visited a strange otherworld of fantasy indeed, namely grandma's attic, a third-hand clothing dispensary, a dime store, and a junkyard! And with these patches and mismatches, this riotous combination of colors and prize collection of trinkets and trash, our attention is noisily solicited, as if something noteworthy were about to take place. It isn't.

The clown will propose to engage in any number of marvelous maneuvers: walk a low-strung tightrope, dive into a bucket, swallow a lighted firecracker, tear a lion limb from limb. But the actual result is little more than a small child could do. And what we find ourselves enjoying about this peculiar fantasy is that the clown has really done nothing fantastic at all. That is the trick, the joke. The clown has abruptly brought us back down from the electrifying world of the high-flying trapeze and the swaying tightrope and the cage of snarling lions to the world of familiar objects, simple accomplishments, and common bumblings. And in this world we discover again a child's delight in life's little bits and pieces.

There are clowns who have used magic, and clowns who have displayed fine musical ability or acrobatic and juggling skill. Bill Rice, the great American clown of the last century, was especially noted for his spellbinding singing of ballads and ditties. The famed English clown Joseph Grimaldi not only sang entertainingly but leaped and somersaulted as few had ever done. And there are many clowns, such as Buster Keaton, who have exercised considerable artistry in falling, running, jumping, climbing, and catapulting. Such nimble and scintillating clowns may move for a time in the direction of pure heroics and artistic genius, but this is always combined with or accompanied by the clown who is a nobody doing nothing special, who makes such a fuss over baubles, the clown who is skilled, if anything, in appearing dense and awkward and clumsy without suffering all the ill effects of such.

The master European clown Grock was such a figure. Though an accomplished musician, he once remarked that the secret of being a good musical clown was that one had to be capable of hitting exactly the wrong note at exactly the right time! In his autobiography, *Life's a Lark*, he defined the special genius of his occupation as that of "transforming the little, everyday annoyances; not only overcoming, but actually *transforming* them into something strange and terrific." It is "the power to extract mirth for millions out of nothing and less than nothing; a wig, a stick of grease paint, a child's fiddle, a chair without a seat."[3] This is the clown's peculiar form of "festivity and fantasy," the real "feast of fools." And the clown's ability to discover some magical transformation in such objects and events presupposes that there is already something strange and terrific about them which we, for all our sophistication, have missed or forgotten.

In Mark Twain's "Which Was the Dream" the narrator of the story has been reading a tale to two children and has suddenly been interrupted. "For ten minutes I had been wandering with these two in a land far from this world; in the golden land of Romance, where all things are beautiful, and existence is a splendid dream, and care cannot come. Then came that bray of brazen horns, and the vision vanished away; we were prisoners in this dull planet again."[4]

But is this intrinsically a "dull planet" in which we are, as it were, imprisoned and from which we must see ourselves as driven to effect an escape—whether into some fantasy of the mind and its creation, or paradise of the imagination, or blissful heaven, or utopian conjecture, or timeless nirvana? Or is this dullness itself a matter of the mode of perception, the dulled art of seeing and savoring? Is not this, in fact, an art that is often dulled by the wandering visions, golden lands of romance, and splendid dreams themselves? Is it not like increasing the amounts of spice added to rice to the point that the rice itself has no taste at all? Or like intensifying the brightness and boldness of colors so much that the subtle differences between muted shadings go unnoticed and become instead so many variants of drabness?

When Chaplin in *The Immigrant*, just off the boat and penniless, manages by a stroke of luck to obtain a plate of plain beans, we are given a lesson in the categories of drabness and dullness. After peering hungrily in the window of a restaurant and emptying his pockets in vain, Charlie discovers a coin on the sidewalk. Though later it turns out to be counterfeit, he joyfully scurries into the restaurant to buy what the coin would buy: a plate of beans. With utmost care he begins by taking each bean, one by one, savoring each tiny morsel, as if it were filet mignon—which to a poor and hungry immigrant is what it was. Similarly, and on another scale, Chaplin in *Modern Times* was able to restore the magic thrill of the most timid kiss or hesitant touch of the hand in befriending an orphan girl, which even the grossest sensualism is incapable of achieving.

While clowns may indulge in the same flights and fantasies as other mortals, exemplifying them and vicariously taking them to ridiculous extremes, impulsively they insist on returning to a defense of the ordinary. And the vicarious extremes are themselves a part of that return. In this manner, attention is called to that perennial human problem in which we become so caught up and imprisoned by our valuational pyramids of important and trivial, brilliant and dullish, beautiful and ugly—in fact a whole thesaurus of antonyms, and gradations between—that much of our experience is turned into a surrounding desert sand. By perceiving things comparatively, even competitively, we develop the habit of looking down upon and dismissing vast areas of potential experience. Instead of savoring beans as beans, we compare them with filet mignon, or at least with jelly beans. We compare them with other beans eaten on some more memorable occasion, or with some fantasy we have of what beans ought to taste like under more ideal conditions, or with those magical beans available only in "Jack and the Beanstalk."

The difficulties are familiar enough. We become so accustomed to the more immediate marvels that surround us that we no longer see them. Or we see them only when they are taken away or become sources of annoyance. We tire of simple pleasures and require new surprises, more superlative creations, greater spectacles, in order to obtain the same sense of thrill, the same delighted wonder, that a small child obtains from sandpiles and rolling balls and cardboard boxes. Each new accomplishment or acquisition becomes in turn the standard that has to be exceeded in order for the elation to continue. The little fifty-cent toy car that captivated the three-year-old boy now costs seven thousand dollars, and perhaps even at that fails to afford the same sense of excitement and wide-eyed enjoyment. We must have more expensive toys, bigger sandpiles, grander plans, larger purposes, higher meanings, even *eternal* significance. Otherwise the world seems to become increasingly flat and tedious and senseless. We begin to think in terms of a new career, a new address, perhaps a new wife or husband. We give serious thought to a change of diet or a change of religion or a change of sex. Perhaps we begin to contemplate timeless essences or suicide or rereading French existentialism and picking up once more the litany of "anxiety," "alienation," "absurdity," "dread," "nausea," and "despair."

This restlessness and disenchantment is usually interpreted religiously as a sign of a restless movement of the spirit, inevitably dissatisfied with "change and decay" or worldly pursuits, which can only exhaust itself and find rest in God—"Our hearts are restless till they find rest in Thee" (Augustine). But there is another way of viewing the matter. Maturity—which is what the seeming immaturity of the clown and fool represents—does not come in an escalation of this process until one collapses in the arms of God or merely in the arms of an ambulance attendant. It comes in a reversal of the process, a de-escalation. Instead of terminating in a kind of cynicism or despair over life, as if caught in a speeded-up merry-go-round from which one yearns to get off, one is reawakened to a new zest for life. Or instead of the world's being scorned in favor of some spiritual regions judged to be eternally satisfying, the world is reopened in its fullness. It is a recovery, at a higher level, of the child's sense of wonder and worth relative to the whole of life, even the slightest particular. One can smell flowers and notice trees, feel water and taste beans, and hear the sound of growing grass once more.

It is the sort of perspective on life that some, like Nikos Kazantzakis's Zorba the Greek, seem never to have lost.

I felt, as I listened to Zorba, that the world was recovering its pristine freshness. All the dulled daily things regained the brightness they had in the beginning, when we came out of the hands of God. Water, women, the stars, bread, returned to their mysterious primitive origin, and the divine whirlwind burst once more upon the air. . . . Everything seems miraculous to him, and each morning when he opens his eyes, he sees trees, sea, stones and birds, and is amazed.[5]

The Child Within

One potential reward of parenthood is being able to discover everything all over again through the eyes of the child. In those enlivening moments the child that we once were, that we have suppressed and all but forgotten, is recollected. But it is no Platonic remembrance of ideal forms, standing serenely behind a world of broken and imperfect reflections. We are given a second look, a re-collection, of all those things that have long since become forgotten in their matter-of-factness. Through the infant's eager gropings and touchings and the child's persistent wonderings and questionings, that which has fallen lifeless is suddenly revived. Even we ourselves enthusiastically begin to point out to the child, and call out the names of, any number of rare phenomena in our immediate surroundings: dogs and cats and rabbits, the birdie and the fishie, the firefly and the moon.

Parenthood is a time in which adults are provided with an opportunity for learning from children. The child has certain secrets on the subject of living, secrets that are shared by clowns and fools and great sages. Except one become like a little child, one cannot enter this kingdom (Matthew 18:3). The child is one who exists in that divine realm which is *prior to* the distinction between marvelous and commonplace, meaningful and meaningless—and all those other categories with which we structure and sterilize our lives. The sage is one who has gone *beyond* the distinction, while the clown is one who *mediates* between the two by garbling the distinction, or in the form of the fool being unable to make the proper distinction. Each in their own way performs that peculiar religious function of treating the marvelous as commonplace, and the commonplace as marvelous, and sensing in everything a great mystery.

From a purely historical standpoint we do not know when the first clown made the first formal appearance. There are scattered pieces of evidence in the ancient world and in modern accounts of tribal societies. But in an informal sense we *do* know, for the original clown is the *child*—the child that we once were and that is still within us, however deeply buried. Children are clowns, and clowns are children, playing on the perimeter of those adult games that we have come to take so seriously that we have forgotten they were games and have lost the spirit of play that first first gave them shape. This is a part of that strange alliance, even conspiracy, between children and clowns over against the sobriety and solidity of the adult world.

Children have a remarkable talent for not taking the adult world with the kind of respect which we are so confident it ought to be given. To the great irritation of authority figures of all sorts, children expend considerable energy in "clowning around." They refuse to appreciate the gravity of our monumental concerns, while we forget that if we were to become more like children our concerns might not be so monumental. There is a certain refreshing element of profanation in the child's world of naiveté and mischief which blows like a gentle breeze through all the stuffy pomposity of adulthood. Often with a simple question or a completely honest remark, perhaps with a quizzical smile or a whimsical laugh, the child can call into doubt the sanctimonious façade and sacrosanct presuppositions of an entire civilization. This too is why the child has always been a major source of inspiration for the clown who self-consciously and ritually reenacts what comes naturally and spontaneously to the child.

The infant, in fact, around the age of one month and well before evidencing any of the more imposing characteristics of humanity—self-awareness, symbolization, speech, reason, abstraction, fantasy, creativity, conscience, responsibility—first of all smiles. *Imago dei*. Up to that point the little creature has given small evidence of being human or of responding to its mother and father in any identifiably human way—even though everyone says it looks exactly like one or both its beaming parents. But then that magic moment comes when the tiny face lights up and the first specifically human response is given. Timid, hesitant, quivering at first, it is the beginning breakthrough in communication—after crying, that is, which it shares with the animals. Shortly thereafter it learns to laugh. It has made the first steps in joining the human race. The time will come when the adult world will try to smother this laughter under a wet blanket of all seriousness and no nonsense. Parents are in such great haste to have their children "grow up" and "get serious" that they are impatient with the carefree, playful world of childish impulse. "Why don't you act your age?" has an all-too-familiar parental ring to it. What is really meant is "Why don't you become more like us?"—that is, nervous, inhibited, anxious, sensitive, grudging, distracted, irritable, bored. William Wordsworth's nostalgic "Recollections of Early Childhood" speaks to the suppression of this world of the child:

> Heaven lies about us in our infancy!
> Shades of the prison-house begin to close
> Upon the growing Boy, . . .
> At length the Man perceives it die away,
> And fade into the light of common day.[6]

Wordsworth's Platonism aside, perhaps this is also a part of that peculiar combination of joy and pathos, laughter and protest, which the clown communicates. The adult world is not all that it was made out to be as we were enticed along, emulating our seniors, unable to wait until we "grew up" and could enter the promised land flowing with milk and honey. Now that we have discovered that this land also flows with Canaanites and Philistines, we cannot go back. "The sadness in legitimate humor consists in the fact that honestly and without deceit it reflects in a purely human way upon what it is to be a child . . . and it is eternally certain that this cannot return." Yet through the presence of clowns and children we *do* go back, we *must* go back, as to the original impulses of our life and joy and laughter.

The clown is the great defender of the world of the child and the spirit of childlikeness. The world of the child is a world of freedom—freedom to laugh and play, to be spontaneous and imaginative, to dance and sing, even the freedom to yell "Ouch" and cry uninhibitedly. It is the world of pure energy, going nowhere in particular and everywhere at once, but above all enjoying the going. It is pure energy expressing itself in the sheer love of being alive and in motion, as if that were enough and the proper end of human life. It is energy bubbling up into giggling and wiggling, teasing and tattling, investigating and wondering, skipping and chattering, all thoroughly thrown into the present moment. It is energy that spills out of and over all those neat distinctions we try to make between holy and unholy, good and bad, valuable and worthless, civilized and savage. This is a part of the energy that the clown taps and dispenses and in turn symbolizes.

The English term clown carries with it some of these same associations and implications. From the time of Elizabethan England, clown meant "clod," "clumsy," "country bumpkin." There was a raw, ruddy earthiness about the figure, a cloddishness. But in this was a kind of childlike innocence and simplicity. In real life the clods were the rough, awkward, unsophisticated farm boys come to the city but bewildered by it, with clothing ill-fitting and perhaps ill-smelling, and certainly at the furthest remove from high fashion and bearing. In their direct manner and unrefined speech they appeared uncouth, rude, and ill-mannered. They were unaccustomed to the decorum—and the deceit—of polite society. They did not "fit in." But because of their innocence of the rules of finery and flattery and their childlike straightforwardness, they could see what others could not see and say what others could not say. Ignorant though they were, they possessed the very virtues that so often get lost in the sophisticated artifice of the city. And by being "beneath it" and "out of it," they were also in a special way "above it all."

The clown thus brings a special truth and spirit that tend otherwise to be suppressed or discounted by those who are more compromised in their existence and more restricted to a certain identity and role. The clod/clown is like the small child in "The Emperor's Clothes" who could both recognize and speak the truth—obvious though it should have been to everyone—that the emperor wore *no* clothes. The child could reveal the "naked truth" because it spoke out of nowhere, as it were, from that no-man's-land that lies outside all conventional adult borders and their ultraserious guardians.

The child is still to a large extent an amorphous creature—just as the clown commonly presents the image of chaos and confusion. Both children and clowns are "lords of disorder," not simply over against order or in the negative sense of corrupting and destroying order, but in the positive sense of returning life to the level of potentiality and freedom. The child is a miniature bundle of endless possibilities, not yet solidly programmed into the language forms and thought structures and myriad other culture patterns that differentiate one human group from another. The child, in the freedom of ignorance and lack of a fixed identity, stands somewhat apart from the social order and all its restrictions and compromises. In this fortunate diplomatic immunity, the child is free to mix things and confuse things and juxtapose things that "don't belong" into fresh and playful combinations.

The child exists in those wonderfully in-between years—as the clown is an in-between figure: in between infancy and adolescence, in between asexuality and puberty, in between innocence and the knowledge of good and evil, in between seriousness and frivolity. Because of this in-betweenness the child and the clown stand also, paradoxically, both between the human and animal sphere on the one hand, and the human and divine sphere on the other. They suggest a mediating category that is not quite human in its innocence and amorphousness and yet more than human in its transcendence of rigid structures and narrow identities. As in the mythical motif of the Divine Child, child and clown seem privy to a higher wisdom and freedom and power. They exist on that border between the preformal and formed, chaos and cosmos, where possibility is unlimited and where the creative spirit broods on the face of the waters. It is a place where things have not yet been sorted out into discriminating categories, and therefore where all things shine with their own peculiar wonderment and fascination.

Paper-bag Mass

A contemporary itinerant fool, Ken Feit, begins his "Fool's Liturgy" with just such a symbolic return to the primordial and the childlike. Sitting cross-legged and barefoot on the floor, plainly dressed in an undershirt and jeans, he puts on the white-face makeup that authorizes him to officiate as fool-priest of the ritual. Carefully he spreads out a cloth as though the floor were his altar. He does not proceed to parody the mass as such. Instead, his movements and his silence evoke a profound sense of reverence and mystery and expectancy. He sets an old brown paper bag before him, like a picnic basket out of which all are to share, at least vicariously, in some fool's feast.

When the crumpled bag is opened, the contents turn out to be nothing much at all: a banana, an apple, a handkerchief, a needle and thread, scissors and paper, a balloon, some molding clay. But as each object is taken from the bag it is greeted with a pantomimed "Wow!" of wide-eyed curiosity and amazement. One is led to suppose that some treasure chest of glittering marvels and choice delicacies is being opened up.

The banana comes first—our kinship with the apes is not forgotten. The banana is examined and fondled and played with as if the fool were a small child discovering all the strange objects of this world from the beginning. One senses the truth in Santayana's dictum that "existence is comic inherently . . . the oddest of possibilities masquerading momentarily as fact."[8] The banana is poked and stroked, tossed in the air, sniffed. It is pinched and pulled at until it begins to peel. A bite is taken, and another bite. The eyes sparkle with delight. Then, after a time, the fool becomes concerned about the banana and attempts to restore it to its former state. Pathetically he pulls upward on the peelings, but they fall back limply. Disappointed, he sets it aside. He senses that he has destroyed something unique and wonderful. Life and death—so much a part of one another.

Like a child, the fool quickly forgets the banana and moves on to examine in turn each of these "oddest of possibilities masquerading momentarily as fact." Finally he decides to return his treasures to their sack. The limp banana comes last. Again he tries to pull it back in shape. It droops forlornly. Then an inspiration strikes him: the needle and thread, of course. Patiently he sews the peelings together. Like a corpse dressed for its casket, the banana is laid tenderly in the bag. Joy and pathos—"yes" is said to both.

In this ritual we are reawakened to that mystery and absurdity and uniqueness that is really there in bananas and apples and balloons and crumpled brown paper bags. Fact is at least as strange as fiction. Reality is as fantastic as fantasy. The fool-priest has recaptured the element of surprise—the essence of both jokes and sacred wonders—

in relation to those things that no longer surprise us. Things begin to jump out at us, strike us as peculiar, incredible, and in their own right fantastic. Once again the oddness of things overwhelms us. The mere act of holding up a banana confronts us with those primordial questions that are at the root of all philosophy and religion: the mysteries of life and death, of matter and time. Why is there something and not nothing? And why this seemingly infinite phantasmagoria of particular things, passing in and out of existence? Why, of all things, bananas? Yet though the oddness and mysteriousness of existence overwhelm us, they do not lead to a sense of bewilderment, nor do they issue in a sense of anxiety or alienation or despair. The context is one of celebration, and the feeling is one of a joyful absurdity in things, a playful surprise, a happy unintelligibility. We are amused. We laugh in awe and wonder. The ordinary world is not very ordinary after all.

Here is the opposite of the magic show. A magician works wonders, elicits "Oohs" and "Ahs," bringing forth rabbits and turtledoves and multicolored scarfs out of an empty bag. The marvel is not in the scarfs or rabbits or turtledoves at all, but in the sleight of hand of the magician. What the fool achieves is the opposite of this. The fool brings forth from a plain shopping bag a beggar's display of the most ordinary objects which, as it were, people everywhere have before them at all times. He carries these about and shows them off as if there were something wonderful about them in themselves. He requires no special magic or miracle, no supernatural wonder or priestly transubstantiation, for bananas and apples and balloons are already experienced as magic and miracle.

Elder Olson defines comedy as the "imitation of valueless action."[9] In one sense this is true, in another sense it quite misses the point. The process is a dialectical one of devaluing the valuable and revaluing the (supposedly) valueless. In the fool's perception lies an ancient wisdom that asserts itself again and again in human history. In relation to the lofty, otherworldly flights of Indian mysticism and mythology that swept into China in the first millennium A.D. came the Zen emphasis upon "nothing special" and "everyday-mindedness." Thus, Master Yun-men defined the spiritual path as "pulling a plough in the morning, and carrying a rake home in the evening." Pao-fu, in response to the question "What is the language of the Buddha?" answered, "Come, let us have a cup of tea!"[10] Lin-chi advised his earnest disciples, "The Way consists of no artificial effort; it only consists of doing the ordinary things without any fuss: going to the stool, making water, putting on clothes, taking a meal, sleeping when tired. Let the fools laugh at me. Only the wise know what I mean. . . . Don't try to be clever and ingenious. Just be ordinary."[11]

Similarly, in relation to the supernaturalism of various forms of Western piety stand figures like Saint Francis of Assisi or Brother Lawrence, for whom the smallest moments and arenas of life had once again become alive and beloved. Or there is Walt Whitman's "Miracles":

. . . I know of nothing else but miracles,
Whether I walk the streets of Manhattan,
Or dart my sight over the roofs of houses toward the sky,
Or wade with naked feet along the beach just in the edge of the water,
Or stand under trees in the woods. . . .[12]

This counterpoint has not been without its instances on the contemporary scene. It is apparent in the recurrent themes of returning to nature and the natural, to the soil, to simpler forms of life, and to the elemental experiences of common people which have manifested themselves in the renaissance of folk music, communes, handcrafting, and classes in organic gardening. It is apparent in those secular gospels that have insisted on reaffirming the integrity of the "profane." It is apparent in that art which is capable of turning even Campbell soup cans into objects of artistic representation (Andy Warhol), or in a music that discovers aesthetic value in common noises and listenings to silence (John Cage), or in a photograph that captures the beauty of doorknobs and cracked walls, driftwood and dandelions, thistles and wrinkled faces (Morton White).

The Spanish painter Joan Miró used to go to the beach to pick up odd bits of things washed up overnight by the tide, take these treasures to his studio, search out their special personality and wonderment, and then rearrange them into some new creation. Similarly, German artist Kurt Schwitters took scraps of this and that—paper, cloth, buttons, tickets, old nails—things discarded, rejected, of no value, rubbish to be turned into a "cathedral." Such an artistic sensitivity—which from the standpoint of "high" art is of course unworthy of the name—is moving in an opposite direction from art that attempts to express the sublime. It is closer to the ridiculous, the absurd, the comic.

Commonplace items are now elevated—like Marcel Duchamp's notorious bottle rack. They are placed on a pedestal and exhibited, surprising and perhaps shocking us, challenging our aesthetic categories, and granted an opportunity to "speak."

This is not an art that attempts to express some ideal attribute or heroic virtue or momentous circumstance in its most glorious form. It does not freeze in a posture of finished perfection instances of youthful beauty, romantic love, patriotic zeal, maternal bliss, or pious devotion. This would be too much like family portraiture, with everyone in the stiffness of Sunday best, properly arranged and unmoving, waiting with twitching smiles for the invisible magic word "Cheese." Such an art inevitably—like such a literature or religiosity—calls forth the comic impulse to tell the rest of the story. It mentions the little matter of twitching and "cheese," displays the rest of the person and the situation, and comes to the defense of lesser forms.

The art of the commonplace is likewise the opposite of that art which, also in flight from the real world and perhaps with some disdain or despair over it, takes delight in abstract forms. The early abstractionist Kasimir Malevich referred to his pioneering black square on white as the result of his "desperate struggle to liberate art from the ballast of the world of objects." The words are remarkably similar to Henri Bergson's description of the Platonic experience of the body as an "irksome ballast which holds down to earth a soul eager to rise aloft." Such an art, and such a spirituality, has difficulty with toy chests and kitchen scenes, street corners and slum-dwellings, barnyards and vegetable gardens—let alone weeds and mice and insects. Alcibiades said of Socrates in the *Symposium*, "Listen to him talk! Why, his language is like the rough skins of the satyrs—nothing but talk of packasses and smiths and cobblers and curriers, and he is always repeating the same things."

The comic protagonist is a defender of all those simple basics of life and survival that tend to be spurned by soaring spirits and heroic visions and wild excursions of fancy. This simplicity is not, however, a rationalization of poverty. Comedy is not, per se, another opiate of the people, a clever strategy for maintaining the status quo by praising dog meat instead of mutton. What is offered is not a religion of the poor, a baked-beans beatitude for Chaplinesque tramps. It represents rather the capacity to enjoy the *whole* of life, including plain beans and rice. Regardless of the fortunes of one's existence, it is the capacity to take pleasure in simple things, common things. And this is a freedom that no amount of increase in one's general welfare can bring.

Tell me, my brethren, what the child can do, which even the lion could not do? Why has the preying lion still to become a child? Innocence is the child, and forgetfulness, a new beginning, a game, a self-rolling wheel, a first movement, a holy Yea.

—Nietzsche, *Thus Spake Zarathustra*[13]

Chapter 5

Will the Real Adam
and Eve Please Stand Up?

There are no lavatories in tragic palaces;
but from its very dawn, comedy had use for
chamber pots.

—George Steiner[1]

One of the problems generated by tragedy, as with "high serious" drama and art generally, is the omission of a considerable amount of relevant detail concerning the total human condition. Such an omission comedy sets out to correct, almost with a vengeance. Tragedy is extremely selective, not only in its representation of human types, but also in the information it admits about even those lives and actions it chooses to dramatize. But comedy introduces whole sets of characters and circumstances, and attitudes and forms of behavior.

In comedy, devoted attention is willingly given to the many particulars of everyday life which a more heroic sophistication seems determined to dress up, cover up, forget, ignore, or otherwise treat as polite unmentionables. The archaic staples of comedy are thus the earthen trinity of sex, food, and body wastes. Added to this are the requirements of clothing, shelter, and sleep—the first two as reminders of our nakedness, the third a reminder of our nightly helplessness and unconsciousness. Mixed in are all those troublesome inevitabilities of burping, itching, scratching, sniffling, twitching, yawning, dozing, stretching, hiccuping, nose-wiping, ear-picking, sneezing, snorting, coughing, choking, spitting, belching, farting—ad infinitum and ad nauseum. There are, indeed, more things in heaven and earth than are dreamed of in our philosophies and theologies!

Already we have much of the basic fare of comic episodes. What, in short, is turned by comedy into a matter of great dramatic consequence is a considerable inconvenience and embarrassment to tragedy. So much is this the case that all this plethora of human activities is almost completely bypassed and suppressed as if such did not, or at least should not, exist.

The Whole Truth

If tragedy deals with more negative and troublesome matters, as it must, it prefers to do so in a grand manner and for some grand purpose. For all its idealism and exalted opinion of the species, tragedy can admit a considerable array of evil and degeneration. Yet it cannot even begin to handle a simple affair like hiccups. When Chaplin in *City Lights* inadvertently swallows a whistle, just as a pompous soloist is beginning to sing, and starts "tweeting" with every hiccup, we know that we are in the world of comedy. Tragic heroes simply don't go around swallowing whistles and "tweeting."

Tragedy will take on any number of bloody battles and fallen houses, but it would be greatly offended at the proposal to pause over a pesky mosquito. It will grant the existence of certain more "noble" weaknesses of the flesh, such as a craving for power, or the love of a beautiful mistress, but it will not touch an inordinate desire for pickles. Tragedy wants to play only with the fine china and silverware, even if it gets stolen or broken in the process. Comedy gets along very well with kitchen spoons, lunch buckets, and eating with impatient fingers.

The comic sense, as Eric Bentley remarks, "tries to cope with the daily, hourly, inescapable difficulty of being." Comedy persists in noticing the little problems of life that are ignored by those who would restrict themselves to major crises and important decisions. If the dramatic hero refuses to acknowledge even such small matters as the necessity of relieving bladder or bowels at the normal time, we are given to understand that a worse fate can occur. Perhaps in the very midst of slaying dragons the hero will be weighed down by constipation! Or in the triumphal procession our hero will begin to squirm uncomfortably in the chariot and smile painfully at the cheering crowds!

The comic perception in this is the protagonist of all that is natural, however ordinary or lowly, while it is the antagonist of all that is unnatural, artificial, affected, or pretentious. Oscar Wilde's aristocratic title *Lady Windermere's Fan* with only slight alteration becomes "Lady Windermere's Fanny"—a less dignified but considerably more fundamental and essential attribute. Kierkegaard had the audacity to note that Hegel, for all his world-historical categories, world-encompassing genius, and grand philosophical system, went like everyone else to pick up his paycheck on Fridays. The list of such comic reminders is unending.

This is not just a matter of debunking. There is in comedy a kind of rock-bottom faith in the essential goodness of what is *natural* to humankind. What is natural is that we should think. And it is equally natural that we should think about eating, sleeping, and sex. What is natural is that we should dream. And what is equally natural is that we must wake up from our dreams, or that if we refuse we shall surely wet the bed. If we bask too long in the sunshine of our createdness in "the image and likeness of God," we will sooner or later be returned to the dust or splattered with mud.

The reasons for tragic delimitations are not hard to come by. Tragedy is inclined not only toward abstracting the more glorious, heroic, and grandly dramatic aspects of human existence, but also toward abstracting spirit from body. The totality of the human condition is avoided as something confusing a singleness of purpose and preventing the exercise and pure nobility of the spirit within. The body gravitates to earth like a great weight, anchoring and restraining a ballooning spirit, eager to make its ascent. The mind soars upward to infinity, the imagination imagines its creative marvels, the spirit floats off toward some limitless bliss, and all the while the body just sits there, finite, lumpy, leaden, and tugging away at the winding-sheet of the ghost within. In the midst of thinking a great thought or dreaming a great dream, we are interrupted by any one of a myriad of petty demands, like a little child insisting on going to the bathroom in the middle of an oratorio.

Such a body easily presents itself as a kind of "tragedy" befallen the spirit, a wart attaching itself to the soul and growing until it encases the "true self" in a ponderous mass. Such a body, so conceived, so tolerated, so used or abused, becomes in Socrates' unfortunate but revealing metaphor "the prison house of the soul." Such a body is worthy of representation at all only in its most ideal, virile, and heroic forms: clothed in great deeds and high drama or frozen in incorruptible marble. Otherwise it is at best a damned nuisance.

This ethereal view of spirit and gross view of body very early becomes comic fare at the hands of Aristophanes, whose *The Clouds* puts Socrates in a basket suspended from a cloud balloon, riding majestically, if precariously, in the sky like a god. When asked what he is doing up there in that curious conveyance, he replies that it is necessary for him to suspend his brain in the sky and mix the essence of mind with that of air, which is of similar nature, in order to contemplate the sun and understand the things of heaven. Had I stayed on the ground, I would have comprehended nothing, for the earth draws to itself the sap of the mind—as is the case with watercress. There follows a discussion of the source of rainfall, the nature of which Socrates understands because his head is in the clouds. His student responds that he always presumed it was Zeus urinating into a sieve. That issue clarified, there still remains the problem of the source of thunder, also attributed to Zeus. Socrates resolves the issue by an analogy with the grumbling stomach that issues in periodic belches: Consider what sounds are produced by the stomach, which is small. Is it surprising that the boundless heavens should produce such loud claps of thunder?

Aristophanes has been much criticized for this attack upon such a paragon of humanistic ideals and philosophical acumen. But it is this very mind/body, spirit/flesh dichotomy with which Aristophanes is dealing. Reason, like the best intentions and highest ideals of tragic aspiration, is not the pure, infallible and trustworthy instrument it often claims to be vis-à-vis the supposed denseness of matter and irrational passions of the flesh. In the hands of a skilled debater or clever defense attorney, and motivated by reward or status or pride or simply the desire to win, reason can be mere sophistry.

By satirizing the "Socratic" training in the sophistic art of "unfair argument," Aristophanes is making the double point that is so much at the heart of comedy. Faith in a reason and virtue somehow emancipated from the restrictions and temptations of the flesh, and returned to the clear light from which it originally came, is unfounded.

Reason is not intrinsically pure any more than the body is intrinsically impure. Reason can confuse, twist, distort, trick, and pervert, just as virtue can become its own downfall. Genius is no more a guarantee of truth than power is a guarantee of justice or a strong will a guarantee of right choice. Thus, as Meredith insisted, "comedy is the ultimate civilizer," not reason or law or moral order.

But the implied derogation of the "impure body" in any attempt at extracting from it "pure" reason and "pure" spirit, and dropping it off like a dirty rag or an outgrown shell, is a lack of appreciation for the integrity of the body and its natural functions. There are times, in fact, when the natural inclinations of the body and the mundane concerns of everyday life are more to be trusted than those principles and visions to which they are sacrificed. One might well argue that the evils resulting from bodily needs and desires per se are nothing in comparison with the evils brought on by reason and imagination—including moral principles, political ideologies, and religious beliefs.

Even greed will preserve that which it has taken by force, whereas ethical, ideological, and religious considerations are often far less merciful. When the prophet Samuel announces to King Saul that God has ordered an attack on the Amalekites to "utterly destroy all that they have" and spare none but slay "both man and woman, infant and suckling, ox and sheep, camel and ass," Saul at least saved the best of the animals on the pretext of offering them in sacrifice (1 Samuel 15). Comedy obeys a different word and a different god and has a different assessment of a reason or righteous spirit that adjusts so well to slaughter. The comic muse might well be more inclined to recommend killing the prophet and sparing the women, children, and camels!

Give Me Your Tired and Your Poor

Comedy goes yet one more step. It points not only to the body but also to bodies of all sorts, from handsome to grotesque. If anything, comedy is focused somewhere between the plain and the grotesque, with some preference for the grotesque. A parade of comic characters would certainly be a motley sight: giants and midgets, the fat lady and the thin man, the rubber-legged and the lame, cross-eyed and cockeyed, the toothy and toothless, the bulbous-nosed and flat-nosed, the blind and deaf, the bald-pated and bushy-haired, the garrulous and tongue-tied—followed by a middling troop of normally unnoticed individuals who are not distinguished in any particular respect. The whole human circus and sideshow is there in comedy, boldly exhibited and trumpeted like some grand human menagerie.

An 1899 Barnum and Bailey Circus poster for "The Greatest Show on Earth" displayed just such an array of assorted people and attractions, along with the title "The Peerless Prodigies of Physical Phenomena and Great Presentation of Marvelous Living Human Curiosities." One of the characteristics that comedy and circus have tended to share is a willingness to encompass and make full use of the whole human spectrum. The costumed beauty rides on the lumbering beast or walks hand in hand with the ugly dwarf. The graceful trapeze artist soars high above the stumbling imitations of the clown in the ring below. Nothing and no one seem to stand outside this circumference, this *circus*.

The motives for inclusion may be mixed. But as even sideshow freaks have often testified, the circus and carnival—like the earlier social niches for fools and grotesques—have been places where they have been wanted and accepted *as they are*. They have been able to hold a job, feel a sense of personal worth, develop friendships, and play a part in this great theatrical mirror-image of human life. Instead of being hidden away in lifelong seclusion, they have been made a focus of special attention. So much was this so at one time, in fact, that circuses had difficulty getting people to move from the sideshow into the main tent—that is until someone at Ringling Brothers came up with the ingenious solution of putting a sign over the exit that read "This Way to the Grand Egress."

When Aristotle classified tragedy with the sublime and beautiful, and comedy with the ludicrous and ugly, there was considerable empirical basis for doing so. Comedy does not restrict itself to, or aim toward, the "best specimens." Any body, and any bodily function or malfunction, that tragedy might spurn as beneath its dignity has been welcomed by comedy with open arms and given a dramatic significance. "Come as you are. Come one and come all." That is the comic invitation and the comic capacity. At the more primitive level, this comic sense may be little more than the combined result of fear of that which is not normal and feelings of superiority over others, along with the necessity of giving some social place to everyone. But the larger result—and at the more sophisticated level, the goal—is that of accepting and admitting this great multitude of human forms, fortunes, and imperfections.

And who would imagine that such delight and camaraderie could be fashioned out of those same abnormalities and subnormalities, or just plain normalities, which otherwise cause such embarrassment, anguish, or boredom! Who would suppose that so much drama could be gotten out of such castoffs as nervous twitches, wobbles, peglegs, and stutterings and stammerings; such miseries as headaches, bellyaches, trips, and falls; such annoyances as seasickness, a stubbed toe, a dropped hammer, or a sudden gust of wind; such miscellaneous occurrences as a tear in the seat of the pants, a butterfly on the nose, pigeon droppings, or an ant in the soup!

Comedy, however, is not just the associate of the ugly and ludicrous. And when Aristotle goes on to argue that tragedy imitates the actions of noble and superior people while comedy imitates those who are ignoble and inferior, one must be careful to note that these are the very values and rankings that are questioned in comedy. The comedian sees the so-called noble and superior person as having an unwarranted vanity and being something of a fool. And there is no fool like a great fool. At the same time, comedy elevates those persons and conditions which, from the standpoint of nobility and superiority, are unworthy of attention—or are worthy only of the attention of ridicule. What comedy proposes is to challenge those very hierarchical valuations that follow from the distinction between noble and ignoble, superior and inferior, sublime and ludicrous, beautiful and ugly. Comedy, by turning attention to all that have been judged to be "beneath us," or beneath those we hold up as exemplars, discovers in these outcasts subjects of special worth and interest.

The comic achievement is quite remarkable. With little to work with in the way of heroes and heroines, fine costuming, labyrinthine plot, profound dialogue, elegant scenery, dramatic action, or casts of thousands, it manages to mesmerize us with life's pots and pans, street scenes, and social rejects. Like so many family and situation comedies, it gets along very well with the kinds of people, petty circumstances, and typical irritations that make up 99 percent of our lives. In fact, the very difficulties and disturbances that in real life may weary us, make us sick, throw us into an outrage, or have us shouting or crying or depressed are transformed by comic ritual into occasions for enjoyment, if not hysterical laughter. This is the ultimate human transubstantiation, the true test of the alchemy of the human spirit. Comedy takes the most common table items of our lives, like bread and wine—items that may also be surrounded by real anguish and suffering—and transforms them into the body and blood of our salvation. The elements remain exactly the same in appearance, yet the inner meaning and outer effect is radically transmuted by a spiritual alchemy from lead into silver and gold.

The miracle of comedy is that what is the source of limitation and dismay to tragic inspiration becomes the source of amusement and celebration. Instead of banging defiantly on the bars of flesh or developing grand schemes of escape, the comedian finds special charm in all the sights and sounds and smells and tastes and touchings within our immediate perception. It is as though in some sacred sense this world for all its inequalities and this body for all its frailties and this time for all its inconsequentia is where one ought to be. It is as though life were intrinsically holy, and that to fail to savor it, rejoice in it, and be humored by it would be a great sacrilege. It is as though we were created out of this dust, to be divided and united as one flesh, and surrounded by this incredible zoo of creatures, both animal and human (Gen. 2). It is as though in some larger sense "God saw everything that he had made, and behold, it was very good [Gen. 1]."

The major task of the comic protagonist, as Nathan Scott insists, "is to remind us of how deeply rooted we are in all the tangible things of this world; he is not, like Shelley or the author of *To the Lighthouse*, a poet of 'unbodied joy.' The motions of comedy, to be sure, finally lead to joy, but it is a joy that we win only after we have consented to journey through this familiar, actual world of earth which is our home." Such is the peculiar but very real salvation that the comedian stoops to bring. It is the comedian who moves within the dustiness and density of the real world, unafraid to get hands dirty and feet muddy, without anxiety over losing face or tarnishing some polished image. "The comedian is not generally an aviator; he does not journey away from this familiar world of earth; he refuses the experiment of angelism; he will not forget that we are made out of dust."[2]

Comedy therefore does not encourage speaking about food and clothing and sex and material things in a hushed voice of apology for the lowly plight the spirit has gotten itself into. Comedy vents our many embarrassments and tensions, and feelings of shame and guilt, in these areas. But the purpose is the opposite of attempting to "liberate" the spirit by disparaging any of the characteristics of human life and thus disabusing the spirit of further interest. Comic simplicity has nothing to do with a righteous beating of the body into numbed submission. Rather, it is an opening up of one's total capacity for wonder and delight, and just plain savoring, in the widest manner possible.

One may of course survey the transciency of things that, despite their transcience, are so frantically desired, clutched, fought over, and even died for. And one may declare them to be nothing in comparison with eternity, or in their vanity unworthy of the wise person's attention. A considerable fool literature has argued the point. In Sebastian Brant's *The Ship of Fools* (1494) this common religious sentiment was characteristically developed:

All things have I recognized as vain, foolish, perishable, doomed soon to slip like water into the earth. Nothing is firm, solid, durable. This brief hour snatches away whatever you may for a short time possess. . . . [O world] I flee you, I leave you, and abandon you completely. And may the gods, and God himself help me, that I may rather prefer to worship you alone, Holy Father, and to follow you, gracious Christ.[3]

Yet time is only a sieve or a sinking ship or a prison if we *choose* to view it that way. Time, as one wit has put it, is simply nature's way of keeping everything from happening all at once.

One may also see in this, for all its apparent piety and sacrifice, a failure to celebrate that form of life given to humanity. In Brant's own religious terms, though life is transient, it is in its very transience holy by virtue of its createdness and givenness. While things may be perishable, it does not follow that they are necessarily vain or foolish. The type of expression represented by Brant has the look of offering creaturely praise and glory to the Creator in preferring "to worship you alone." But it is actually a lament against the Creator and creation. The world is piously despised as unworthy of human affection. It is as if to suggest that we had been cheated and betrayed by the ephemerality and imperfection of life. It is, in fact, as if we were much too noble for a world where things are constantly breaking, decaying, dying, and otherwise confounding and disappointing us.

A good deal of rebellion and complaint has been passed off in this manner as thanksgiving and devotion. And the confusion is considerably aided by doctrines of some original paradise, on earth or in the heavens, where matters were not so and from which we have fallen or been evicted. Ergo, the cultivation of whining or disgust is not only permissible, it is a religious virtue—or, in other mythological circles, a mark of existential authenticity.

Yet the evil is not in time and matter. The evil is in that very salvation which would measure time by eternity and matter by spirit. The beauty of matter is that it is so material. The beauty of time is that it is just like time. The beauty of change is that it is so changeable. Plum blossoms and cherry blossoms, as the Japanese have appreciated almost to the point of a national passion, are beautiful despite the fact, and in a sense because of the fact, that their beauty is so fragile and brief. Thus Kenko could write, "If man were never to fade away like the dews of Adashino, never to vanish like the smoke over Toribeyama, but lingered on forever in the world, how things would lose their power to move us! The most precious thing in life is its uncertainty."[4]

If one judges an old, cracked, misshapen tea bowl, with its irregular coloration and happenstance configurations, by the standards of finely detailed and lacquered porcelain, it may appear ugly. And yet it is highly prized, for that which is old and worn, that which is imperfect and unfinished, that which is off-center and asymmetrical and accidental, has a special beauty all its own. And no image of its opposite can ever negate that beauty. If anything, it can only enhance it by comparison. The old, rough, irregular tea bowl is of great value precisely because it is *not* new, symmetrical, and finished to perfection.

Though nothing in this life is "firm, solid, durable," it does not follow that its elements are "vain, foolish, and doomed." What is vain is to imagine things to be otherwise, and to lament the fact that they are not. Fleeing from such a perishable and imperfect world is the very foolishness from which the clown and comedian would save us. The idea of paradise is itself the fall.

The Comic Mean

While the tragedians are representing humanity in terms of gods and kings (Prometheus, Oedipus, Lear), the comedians often counter by using animals (Aristophanes' *Birds, Frogs,* or *Wasps*). It should be emphasized, however, that comedy does not point only to flesh and finiteness and dustiness. Since what comedy chooses to portray is usually what has been omitted, its content has some dependence upon whatever the omission of the day. This does not mean that comedy is parasitic, but rather that its task is one of counterbalancing and mediation. It is there to tame the beast or tie down the angel in us, whichever is parading at the moment. Comedy is a moderator of passions, both subhuman and superhuman. It is the restorer of unity and wholeness.

One thing that is so often missing, whether in the ritual arena or in everyday life, is the *spirit* which comedy represents: laughter, lightheartedness, playfulness, gaiety, frivolity. And that spirit it insists upon, whatever the subject matter or concern. But the *form* and *content* of comedy may differ considerably, depending on what has been omitted. Commonly what is missing is a full recognition of human limitations and hence a sense of perspective relative to those lofty portraits and painted pretensions with which we flatter ourselves. So comedy displays our finiteness, our foolish bunglings, our phallic fantasies, our lustings after power.

But if the prevailing portrayal is reversed, and humanity and human relationships are in danger of reduction to the physical level or of being deluged by dirt and smut, comedy can recoil and parody this as well. The human animal who seems to be all muscle or all stomach or all sex organs can be just as comical as someone who seems to be all brain or all talk or all-important. The monkey, the pig, the cock, the ass—these are stock figures in comedy which not only call attention to our kinship with the animal kingdom but also remind us that we are something more than monkeys, pigs, cocks, and asses. We are something more even in the act of trying to reduce ourselves to these dimensions.

Comedy is not, therefore, to be identified simply with earthiness, for in content it is not necessarily focused on sensuality any more than on spirituality, the realities of matter any more than those of mind. Obviously there are follies of the body as well as of the mind. The point that comedy succeeds in making emphatically is that human nature is *both* mind and body. And in its insistence on both is its defense of the whole person, the fully human.

Implicit in this defense is thus a repudiation of the illusory separation of spirit from body in the first place. And here we note an intriguing affinity with a wholistic biblical anthropology, vis-à-vis all "ghost-in-the-machine" dualisms. The body is not seen as "inhabited" by some fallen bird of paradise, trapped in a cage of matter and flesh from which it flees every chance it can get and perhaps hopes eventually to flee altogether. The distinction between spirit and body is seen as a deceptive distinction made possible by a periodic forgetfulness of the body, lost in thought or transported in imagination. Spirit and flesh, mind and body, are convenient fictions for pointing to aspects of what is fundamentally one person. The comic reminder of this is in itself an important religious function. The comic perception is that of a basic unity of "spirit" and "flesh" which become two by a process of mental abstraction from the whole person.

This perception is already announced in one of Aristophanes' early comedies, *The Acharnians* (425 B.C.):

Here I contemplate, here I stretch my legs;
I think and think—I don't know what to think.
I draw conclusions and comparisons,
I ponder, I reflect, I pick my nose,
I make a stink; I make a metaphor,
I fidget about, and yawn and scratch myself.[5]

While a more noble and heroic image of the species would wish to limit the list of human attributes and activities and extract pure thought or pure spirit from its distractions, in comedy all this is perceived as the activity of *one* person. Contemplating and stretching, thinking and yawning, making a metaphor and making a stink are not only intermingled but finally inseparable. In alluding to this, however, and making some sport of it, comedy is not ridiculing the life of the mind per se. Rather, it is ridiculing the presumption that the life of the mind exists apart from and in abstraction from the totality of one's being. For all its iconoclasm, there is in comedy an underlying affirmation of the sacredness and worth of the whole of life.

To this point there is an agreement with those mystical visions of unity in which the human problem is seen as having something to do with the separation and alienation of one thing from another. But comedy is inclined to include among these divisive factors those very categories that are so often used in trying to transcend the problem: spirit and flesh, mind and matter, eternity and time, being and becoming. Instead of proposing to resolve the difficulty by attempting to turn attention increasingly away from the "imperfect" and fragmented forms of matter to the "perfect" and unbroken forms of mind, the comic solution is to transcend the distinctions themselves. As John Dominic Crossan has argued, "the range of comic play extends from the scatological to the eschatological. I would even suspect that the greatest comedy is that which fuses together 'low' and 'high' comedy, scatology and eschatology, into a transcending unity."[6]

From the comic perspective, the world of illusion and delusion from which we are to be delivered is not this world of space, time, body, and matter. It is the world that separates and estranges spirit from body, mind from matter, sacred from profane and sets up a series of gradations from one category to the other. Comedy does not encourage flight into some ethereal realm of pure ideas, ideal forms, or floating spirits, any more than it encourages flight into gross sensuality and pure animality. Despite its gleeful delight in openly displaying the awkwardness of our being, comedy throws us into the zaniest contradictions as a reminder of our many-sided complexity and as a mock prelude to uniting us again.

As William Lynch has put it, "to recall this incredible relation between mud and God is, in its own distant, adumbrating way, the function of comedy."[7] Did even Plato entertain this possibility in the end? Perhaps, if Nietzsche's "happily preserved *petit fait*" is correct, "that under the pillow of his deathbed there was found no 'Bible,' nor anything Egyptian, Pythagorean, or Platonic, but a volume of Aristophanes."[8]

The Mystical Cat

Religions are often credited with contributing to the problem by dazzling the minds of devotees with ecstatic experiences, promises of bliss in heaven or nirvana, images of lost paradises and paradises to come. And often it is correct that religions become supply houses for mythologies of disenchantment and rituals of disengagement. The problem is well illustrated from an incident in the life of the nineteenth-century Hindu sadhu Ramakrishna, who from childhood had manifested a tendency to pass into trances. The tendency was accentuated during his later priesthood to the point that he once went into *samadhi* for six months, kept alive only by the grace of an attendant who forced food and water into his mouth and cleaned up his body wastes.

62336

During one such period, Ramakrishna was performing the prescribed morning ritual before the altar of the goddess Kali, and as frequently would happen, partway into the chant he began to have visions. Everywhere he looked he saw Mother Kali: the stone image, the altar, the water vessels, the marble floor, the open doorway, a worldly passerby outside the temple. All became so many forms of the goddess. Just at that moment a stray cat wandered into the temple, meowing hungrily. Ramakrishna, hearing the cry as the voice of Kali calling to him, took the consecrated food from the altar and set it on the floor for the cat. Also at that moment the overseer of the temple had entered the sanctuary and, shocked by Ramakrishna's sacrilege, demanded an explanation for his conduct. Ramakrishna replied innocently that he had had a vision of the presence of the goddess in everything and that when he had heard the goddess meowingly imploring him to give her the food, he had done so. [9]

In one sense this is very much akin to a scene replayed again and again in the history of the comic tradition. Something holy is profaned (sacred food), and something profane is elevated and treated as holy (a common cat). Customary expectations are overturned, and established categories are jumbled or reversed. But the case of Ramakrishna's cat is only a partial success, and the reasons for this are quite revealing of the religious problem of spirituality and ecstasy. Though the story is not lacking in humor, something is missing. And essentially what is missing is the cat.

This question immediately presents itself: Would Ramakrishna in a normal state of consciousness have given the offering to the cat? Would Ramakrishna have been willing to offer the food to the cat *as a cat*, in fact, the most profane form of cat (an alley cat), rather than as a form of the goddess? Would Ramakrishna have had compassion on the cat because the *cat*, inconsequential and lowly though it was, was hungry and begging for food? Or has not Ramakrishna, in the very act of endowing this common cat with the supreme value of being an embodiment of the goddess, emptied the cat of any intrinsic value it may have had by virtue of simply being a cat? It is as if being a cat is not enough to qualify for attention or compassion or sacred food.

In this case the separation between sacred and profane has been overcome by ignoring and annulling the profane in an ecstatic transformation of the cat into something else, albeit the sublime presence of the All-Mother. What is now of value is not what the cat is in itself as a cat—in fact, in its own unique individuality as this particular cat—but as an empty vessel for some universal divine reality. And relative to this ultimate reality, this pathetic stray cat, already near the bottom of the scale of values and hopelessly profane, can now only appear as nothing, a hollow shell, an apparition in the illusory world of *maya.*

At this point the comic tradition parts company with those mysticisms that place a premium on ecstatic oceans of bliss and transcendent unities of being, relative to which the spheres of ordinary consciousness, everyday concerns, and individual uniquenesses are downgraded, if not declared to be fallen and unenlightened levels of perception. Like mysticism, comedy aims at overcoming dualities, breaking down walls that separate one thing from another. It juxtaposes opposites as a means of softening the opposition, establishing a sense of the feeling, "We're all in this together." But it does so by challenging our hierarchies of value as well, which also separate one thing from another or deceptively unite things by reducing them to something else.

Comedy liberates us from those boxes in which we isolate and insulate ourselves, and from those grading systems in which we make ourselves out to be superior or inferior. But it does not then dissolve individual difference and separate worth in some ultimate oneness that alone, or even supremely, is holy, true, good, and beautiful. Comedy continues to wonder about cats.

Chapter 6

Between Dreams and Dust

I have seen everything that is done under the sun; and behold, all is vanity and a striving after wind.

—Ecclesiastes 1:14

A popular television program of the 1960s, *Candid Camera*, advertised itself as specializing in the humorous circumstances of "people caught in the act of being themselves." Among the seemingly inexhaustible situations of candid comedy was an episode in which an aptitude test had been given to the graduating seniors of a select eastern prep school. *Candid Camera* personnel, in the guise of evaluators of the tests, interviewed some of the students. In one interview, two young men had been called in to receive a firsthand report of the findings. Both were honor students with college and professional futures clearly on their minds. In a very dramatic and enthusiastic tone, the bogus evaluators indicated that after careful examination of the aptitude scores they were pleased to announce the results in person. The tests showed conclusively that the young men were especially well suited to being shepherds!

The look of astonishment and consternation was priceless—both for its comic effect and for its indication of our contemporary distance from the pastoral tradition. While the shepherd and sheep, as well as the Adam and Eve of the shepherd's mythology, are prominent images in the religious heritage of Western civilization, they are so remote from most moderns as to be almost unthinkable. The kind of experience and outlook that the shepherd represents is nevertheless available to us, both as a problem that will not leave us and as a perspective symbolized for us in other forms. One of these is that of the comic tradition itself, particularly that of the nonhero.

The nonhero is one who stands, by and large, outside the great powers and competing forces of the day and who from the standpoint of these movers of history is literally quite "out of it"—much like the contemporary Bedouin tribesmen in the Middle East who live in the same hard and happy simplicity on the desert fringes of "where the action is," as have their goat- and sheep-herding forebears for several millennia. Yet the nonhero represents certain truths about ourselves which are as universal as the truths they counterbalance. The nonhero is "out of it" in the same sense children and clowns and fools seem "out of it," yet privy thereby to a larger wisdom.

The Recovery of Simplicity

Sometimes one has to turn to children's tales for this wisdom. In Munro Leaf's now classic story of Ferdinand the bull,[1] we find an especially charming modern instance of the nonheroic type and its own peculiar comic perspective on human nature and destiny. The bull is the great ancient symbol of masculine virility and ferocity. He is strength and war and blood and sex in heroic proportions. But young Ferdinand was no ordinary bull. Ferdinand had no interest whatsoever in running and jumping and butting heads like all the other adolescent bulls in the Spanish countryside. He just liked to sit under his favorite cork tree and smell flowers. To accentuate the anomaly further, as the years went by Ferdinand grew into a very large, very strong bull. Still he preferred his cork tree and flowers to the tests of valor that were fashionable among the other young bulls who hoped to fight in Madrid.

On the basis of this comic inversion, the story proceeds. One day five men came scouting for the most splendid and spirited bulls for the bullring. All the other young bulls began to run about, challenging and charging and putting on their fiercest display. But not Ferdinand. He ambled across the pasture to sit under his tree and watch others impress the scouts. But when Ferdinand went to sit down, to his misfortune he sat on a bumblebee and was stung, whereupon

Ferdinand jumped up with a great roar and began running about wildly, snorting and bellowing, butting the air and pawing the ground in a most impressive manner. And when the five scouts saw the performance, they all exclaimed that Ferdinand was clearly the most ferocious bull of the lot. So they took him away in a cart to Madrid.

Suddenly Ferdinand had been awakened from his Edenic bliss. His tree had become a Tree of Knowledge. In heroic terms[2] the "call to adventure" had been given. And while he had at first "refused the call," now fate had thrust it upon him. He was transported out of his pastoral paradise into the very center of urban life. There he was to play the ritual role of the hero in a tragic fight to the death with another hero, the bullfighter.

On the day of the bullfight a huge crowd was assembled, all expectantly awaiting Ferdinand, who was said to be one of the mightiest bulls ever to have been brought to the arena. When the gate was opened Ferdinand walked out to the center of the ring to the wild cheers of the crowd. But when Ferdinand got to the center of the ring, he looked around and saw all the beautiful flowers in the hair of all the beautiful ladies. And he just sat down in the middle of the ring to enjoy them. No matter what the matador and the picadors did, no matter how unmercifully they poked him and jabbed him and shouted at him, they could not get Ferdinand to fight. So they had to take him back to his pasture, where he sits to this day under his favorite cork tree, smelling flowers.

While Leaf's story uses some of the same patterns and themes as other heroic tales, it abruptly and humorously moves in an opposite direction. And the heroic values and virtues are completely reversed. Proponents of the "monomyth" of the hero might attempt to classify Ferdinand as a variant of the universal type.[3] But Ferdinand is clearly no hero. He is the antithesis of the hero. And if there is an archetypal image of the hero embedded somewhere deep in our psyche, here is clear testimony to a counter-archetype, with its own parallel validity.

If anything, Ferdinand is more like the lackluster Adam and Eve of Genesis, who organized no grand rebellion against the gods and made no defiant assault on the heavens or clever steal from divine altars, but who quite unheroically got talked into eating some forbidden fruit in a conspiracy of circumstances. We are in the world of pastoral simplicity. But the questions being raised are still the same basic questions: What is human nature and destiny, and where is true life to be found? And they are being answered from the peculiar standpoint of the nonheroic delight in the ordinary.

For most of Ferdinand's friends, life was to be found in Madrid, in the bustle of the city, the expectation of new excitements, the adventure of the ring, the thrill of competition, the cheering of the crowds, the heroism of the contest, the valiant fight to the death. But for Ferdinand there was something very special and enchanting in all those common things immediately about him in his humble pasture, like cork trees and grass and flowers and the occasional gyrations of a butterfly—excepting, of course, bumblebees. If his companions lived in the push-and-pull world of a "yang" aggressiveness, Ferdinand understood the strength and beauty of a "yin" passivity: stillness, tranquillity, immediacy, nonstriving.

A story like this cuts deeply against the grain of the kind of "bullishness" that characterizes civilizations and their enterprises. It seems particularly subversive of the progressivist mythology of "onward and upward forever" that has dominated the modern West and now seems destined to dominate the whole world. To such an ideology of competition and advancement, Ferdinand cannot help but evoke images of lazy bums, loafers, the clods who will never get anywhere or make anything of themselves. He has no stirring sense of vision, no grand scheme, no consuming passion. Ferdinand is not even *tempted* to leave Eden. He has to be thrown out. And even when thrown out and dazzled by the progress of the city and cast into the midst of an electrified mob and egged on by every conceivable enticement and prodding, he sits down and insists on turning the bullring into a pasture.

Ferdinand is no hero, but he is a very remarkable bull. He has none of those dramatic qualities that would attract the attention of pioneering, competitive, and conquering temperaments, and he performs none of those marvelous feats that might give him a name and turn him into a stirring legend. He climbs no mountains, plunges into no watery abysses, slays no dragons, rescues no maidens, outwits no gods or demons, and lays claim to no saving discoveries. Yet one suspects that in a peculiar manner all his own he is already where the hero is trying so valiantly to get.

It would be only too easy to dismiss this as a romantic pastoralism or primitivism, or a nostalgic regression to a child's Garden of Eden. And both Marxists and capitalists could cry, "Palliative for the masses." But such would miss the more subtle and more mature perceptions being symbolized. Alien though this may be to the official cultural image of ourselves as the doers of great deeds and the shapers of some "manifest destiny," there is a certain wisdom here. It is a wisdom that finds contentment in the familiar periodicities of life: the ceaseless round of day and night, the waxing and waning of the moon, springtime and harvest, the encircling years, the day-by-day repetitions which never get anywhere and in which there is "nothing new under the sun."

Comedy has always fit in well with the natural and biological rhythms of life. It moves with special ease among the perennial themes of children, love, sex, marriage, food, drink, sleep. It welcomes without cynicism and without weariness those successive waves of blossoming trees and nesting birds and young lovers in which the same old process repeats itself for the trillionth time, yet in each instance as if for the very first time.

The comic image of time is not that of a spiral staircase to the stars. Time is cyclical, liturgical, and centered in the present. Its sense of space is likewise "present," as if one need not build high towers to the heavens or journey to the center of the earth or make pilgrimage to some holy city in order to gain meaning, worth, and direction. One is already *there*. And relative to this sense of arrival, heroic quests have the appearance of grand detours, romantic distractions, perhaps even impending disasters. As Joseph Meeker has commented,

to people disposed in favor of heroism and idealistic ethics, comedy may seem trivial in its insistence that the commonplace is worth maintaining. The comic point of view is that man's high moral ideals and glorified heroic poses are themselves largely based on fantasy and are likely to lead to misery or death for those who hold them.[4]

The Clever Man and the Simple Man

This comic point of view is quaintly articulated in the Yiddish tale of the Clever Man and the Simple Man.[5] According to the tale, two neighboring sons have been orphaned. The one is clever, the other simple. The clever son sells his father's property and goes off to seek his fortune. His considerable intelligence and skill give him resounding success in everything he tries. He masters not only the world of trade and finance, but also the science of medicine, the art of sculpture, and the craft of the goldsmith. But the same lofty standards and high ambitions that have carried him to a surpassing excellence in every endeavor leave him perpetually dissatisfied with others and with himself. The least imperfection infuriates him, and the perfection of his accomplishments bore him once they are achieved, endlessly causing him to search out new worlds to conquer, which in turn bore him when conquered.

The simple son remains in his father's house and becomes a shoemaker. He is not perpetually imagining new forms of life for himself, but is quite satisfied in being a simple shoemaker. He becomes, in fact, a rather poor shoemaker; his shoes come out looking like triangles! Yet though he is without special talent and accomplishment, and though he is poor and life is hard, he takes great pleasure in what little he has. He eats bread as if it were roast beef and drinks water as if it were fine wine. He lives and enjoys each day as it comes and in the form in which it comes.

After many years, the king, having heard of these opposite types and desiring to meet them, sends a summons to each. The clever son, clever as always, scrutinizes the summons and its messenger. This might not be from the king at all, and no one is going to fool him or make a fool of him. He has always gotten the better of everyone and every situation and is not about to be duped now. So he refuses to go. The simple son, however, goes immediately. And when the king sees what a simple person he is, and how little he is concerned about cleverness or power or wealth or ambition or self-importance, he makes him his chief minister.

A similar wisdom was expressed by an eighth-century Chinese sage, Layman P'ang:

How wondrous this, how marvelous!
I carry fuel, I draw water!

The poem, brief as it is, manages to contain a very odd mixing of terms. We are hardly inclined to think of such daily tasks as carrying wood and buckets of water as being particularly wondrous or marvelous, let alone "meaningful." This despite the fact, and perhaps because of the fact, that most of life consists of such inconsequential and recurrent events, just as most of human labor is menial and repetitive. It is possible that an advancing senility had dimmed P'ang's powers of discrimination between significant and insignificant duties. And it is conceivable that Layman P'ang suffered a severe blow on the head the week before and ever since had been confusing categories like "marvelous" and "ordinary." But it is also possible that he had touched on the delicate inner secret of carrying fuel and drawing water, a secret that is the special wisdom of small children and great sages as well as simple fools.

It is a secret than an age, like ours, of great sophistication and great achievement, and consequently also of jaded sensibilities, has some difficulty in grasping. Our search after the wondrous and marvelous is everywhere *but* in the simple acts of carrying fuel and drawing water. For us the ecstatic moment is to be found where the term itself literally suggests it is to be found: in *ecstasis*, standing outside, going beyond, being beside oneself.

The ecstatic quest has really become the overpowering myth of our time, the Holy Grail of both our most sublime aspirations and most subliminal forms of abandon. That which is Real, that which makes life worth living or at least endurable, is to be found up there or down there, back there or out there, on some far perimeter of existence, beyond the dull, trivial, boring, humdrum recurrences of life.

Herbert Read's description of one of the impulses of fantasy in modern art is a typical modern restatement of the problem rather than its solution: "The inner world of the imagination becomes more and more significant, as if to compensate for the poverty and drabness of everyday life."[6] The imagination is, of course, capable of proposing endless other worlds, more paradisal or monstrous, or at least more exciting and challenging, than the current one. In this lies both the strength and weakness of fantasy. By means of a cultivated dissatisfaction with whatever forms of life are immediately available, everyday life becomes a matter of poverty and drabness, whether it is or not, and even for those who live in the palaces of other people's imaginations.

One is perpetually led to suppose that true satisfaction and true being and truth itself are somewhere else. Life is therefore, like Plato's cave, seen as so many shadows cast by the real and forgotten radiance beyond. Or, like *Pilgrim's Progress*, life is turned into a tortuous, labyrinthine pilgrimage to some distant City of Light. Existence is always being postponed and awaited: at the end of the tunnel, over the last mountain, beyond the far horizon. And all immediate circumstances are ignored or despised or turned into so many stepping-stones to the grand kingdom of elsewhere.

In a sense, it makes little difference whether this magical-mystical-mysterious moment is imaged in terms of the heroism of soaring flight (eagles and hawks) or subterranean descent (serpents and frogs). It makes little difference whether the desired goal is envisioned in terms of the eurekas of scientific discovery, space conquests, and technological wonders; or in terms of the triumphs of market coups, military supremacy, and sexual exploits; or in terms of the paradises of revolutionary utopias, otherworldly mysticisms, or heavenly abodes. In structure and spirit the questings are quite similar—hence the plausibility of a mono-mythology of the hero. Vitality, Completeness, Fulfillment, Real Life—these are not to be found among the immediate circumstances of life, but in transcending them or escaping from them or in that peculiar form of excess, *exceeding* them. And the end result is also much the same. Instead of being revitalized, the world of the commonplace is rendered even more commonplace.

Transcending Sacred and Profane

Understandings of the sacred have also tended to parallel this understanding of the ecstatic, if they are not partly the result of it. That which is sacred is that which "confronts," "breaks into," or "intersects" an otherwise profane space and time, lacking in meaning, value, and direction. The sacred is that which has been *ecstatically* perceived through some flight of the soul or in-breaking revelation. And this holy vision comes bringing meaning, value, and direction to what otherwise is only a "booming, buzzing confusion."

Mircea Eliade in volume after volume has repeated this theme: "The first possible definition of the sacred is that it is the opposite of the profane." The sacred is that "manifestation of something of a wholly different order, a reality that does not belong to our world, in objects that are an integral part of our natural, 'profane,' 'profane' world."[7] Eliade has also insisted that a fundamental characteristic of religion is the "nostalgia for paradise," the desire to live as much as possible in this sacred, ideal world. Myth and ritual, accordingly, provide an "escape from time" into a primordial-eternal moment, and a release from the "terror of history" into the secure and meaningful world of ahistorical archetypes.

But if the first principle of religion is the separation of sacred and profane, there is also a second principle, which is the reverse, or reversing, of the first: the *overcoming* of the distinction between sacred and profane, meaningful and meaningless. It is the return to this immediate, ordinary world of "profane" interests, objects, and events in renewed fascination. While there are those ecstatic moments in which we stand outside, are called outside, or are thrown outside the realm of everyday experience, there are also those "enstatic" moments in which we stand more deeply within and are compelled to reaffirm and revitalize the realm of everyday experience itself.

In this countermovement is a perception of the ambiguity of the sacred which, though it may be seen as that which gives meaning and value to the profane sphere that surrounds it, by its very separateness and elevation tends to *empty* the profane sphere of significance and worth. We are confronted by the paradox that the sacred *creates* the profane. As a result, offering itself as the ultimate basis of being and salvation, the sacred may become the place of hiding, evasion, and retreat, a templed refuge from life rather than a restoration of it. Or it may become the denial of life, the negation of this world as hopelessly profane, from the snares and illusions of which one is now to be rescued. Or, in revolt against either of these results, the sacred may elicit a defiant emptying of the heavens and repudiation of all sacrality in favor of secularity in a death of all gods.

Here is one of the important sources of all those comic rituals that profane holy things. As a means of revaluing what has tended to become devalued, the comic officiant boldly touches in a profane manner that sacred object which is not to be touched, then turns around and treats with great reverence something that is normally considered profane. This elevation is not simply a mock reverence, but a perception of an intrinsic value which has been overshadowed or suffocated. The clown and fool profane holy things so that the holiness of profane things might be revealed.

When the Zen master Bankei was preaching a sermon one day, he was interrupted by a zealous Shin-shu priest. The priest challenged him to authenticate his teaching by pointing to some significant accomplishment or by performing the kind of miracle attributed to the founder of the Shin (True) sect. Bankei replied simply, "Perhaps your fox can perform that trick; but that is not the manner of Zen. My miracle is that when I feel hungry I eat, and when I feel thirsty I drink!"[8] What indeed could be more wondrous and marvelous than this,—except that our sensitivities have been dulled to the mystery?

The usual religious assumption is that mystery and miracle belong to the extraordinary and that it is in those dramatically, perhaps traumatically, supranormal experiences that awe and wonder are evoked. A divine reality is sought in some earthshaking event or transfiguring vision, when all life is a marvel and the tiniest creature an unfathomable mystery. Karl von Frisch put the point in a more "profane" and amusing manner.

The layman may wonder why a biologist is content to devote fifty years of his life to the study of bees and minnows without ever branching out into research on, say, elephants, or at any rate the *lice* of elephants. . . . The answer to any such question must be that every single species of the animal kingdom challenges us with all, or nearly all, the mysteries of life.[9]

Part of the difficulty is that we often live in such a prosaically matter-of-fact, mere-noticing acquaintance with the life about and within us that we need, or feel we need, something of the magnitude of a herd of elephants to awaken our consciousness. Like Moses, we require a special flaming bush that miraculously is not consumed in order to command our attention. Or, tiring of the flatland of our experience, we set off into the mountains to wait for lightning to strike us from above and to be jolted by some thundering voice of God. But important as such experiences might be, the result is often like staring at the sun: we are blinded to the profundity in simple things. The "flatland" from which we have been rescued looks ever flatter by comparison. And the thunder at the mountaintop deafens us to the still, small voices in the valley below.

In religious experience, there seem to be two directions that may be taken relative to the boredom, the *ennui*, that overtakes our lives. The one direction is to seek for some new experience that is elevating and exhilarating and that gives a thread of meaning and value to life. The other is to reawaken to the intrinsic meaning and value we once found in the simplest, most familiar things. The differences between these two paths are akin to William James's distinctions between twice-born and once-born religious experience.[10] The twice-born, having fallen into a soul-sickness and world-weariness where life has lost color and significance, doubts assail from all directions, and perhaps in despair suicide is even contemplated as the heroic way out, are rescued from this dungeon by some enthralling experience that suddenly gives a sense of release and redirection. But the once-born, living in the grace of what James called "healthy-mindedness," rarely stray very far from the simple joys of life and do not get carried off into the depths of depression, doubt, and despair. Since they never fully lose the pristine, childlike sense of marvel and delight in the world they occupy, they are not so inclined to search out new worlds or scale emotional precipices, but rather seek to be reawakened and revived. Thus while the watchwords of the twice-born are regeneration, rebirth, or revolution, those of the once-born are renewal and revitalization.

One characteristic of biographies of the twice-born is that they make good stories—which is also the reason they tend to predominate in religious literature: Moses, Mohammed, Buddha, Paul, Augustine, Luther, Pascal. Unlike the more commonplace biographies of the once-born, if they are reported at all—and they usually are not—they make for good press and good theater. There are dramatic conflicts, emotional extremes, dark passions, and deep depressions. There are powerful temptations to overcome, tortuous ordeals to be passed, mental abysses and physical snake-pits to fall into. And when light and liberation come, they are often haloed in extraordinary sensations, supranormal visions, ecstatic transports, altered states of consciousness, bliss.

Abraham Maslow, using a similar distinction between "peakers" and "nonpeakers," likens such peak experiences to "a visit to a personally defined Heaven from which the individual then returns to earth."[11] Such an experience may leave the individual "loving, unconcdemning, compassionate and perhaps [with an] amused acceptance of the world."[12] But it may also leave the individual more impatient and uncompromising with the mundane world and those who seem easily satisfied with its menial pursuits. And while so sublime an experience may lead to the greening of the former desert of one's existence, it may also leave it more deserted by comparison with more heavenly joys. The experience may then become an end in itself rather than a means of restoring the joy of life, so that everything else is set aside in favor of its remembrance or sacrificed to its hoped-for repetition. "The peak experiences of pure delight are for my subjects among the ultimate goals of living and the ultimate validations and justifications for it."[13]

Yet the problem remains: How can *everything* be perceived as a legitimate end in itself, however lowly, insignificant, plain, or profane? How can everyday life in itself be special and sacred? The answer to this lies in the peculiar wisdom granted to the simpleton who has but one grace to offer: the humble enjoyment of simple things.

Sometimes it takes a skirmish with death or serious illness to recover this perspective on life. It was a position to which Maslow himself came near the end of his life, when his busy professional career was abruptly halted by a near-fatal heart attack. He later commented,

One very important aspect of the post-mortem life is that everything gets precious, gets piercingly important. You get stabbed by things, by flowers and by babies and by beautiful things—just the very act of living, of walking and breathing and eating and having friends and chatting. Everything seems to look more beautiful rather than less, and one gets the much-intensified sense of miracles.[14]

It is unfortunate that such a revelation often comes only at the end of one's life rather than at the beginning—though in a sense it *is* given in the beginning, as the once-born best understand, but is left to "die away," and fade into the light of common day."

Ironically, it was Maslow who had given the highest marks to "peakers" as the most mature, self-actualized, fully developed, highly evolved human beings—just as James credited the twice-born with the greatest depth, sensitivity, richness, and completeness. Perhaps it is not entirely inappropriate to suggest that a heart attack qualifies as a peak experience. But if so, it is not a peak experience that dulls all other experiences by comparison or that seeks to recapture itself in prayers for repeated peaks. One of the distinct advantages of a heart attack is that one is not inclined to make of it an end in itself. A heart attack can be only one thing: a jolt, a bit of internal shock-therapy, awakening one to what had always been there, readily available, but unnoticed or only half-noticed in that dim awareness of the present moment.

Beyond Oedipus, Dionysus, and Apollo

When one speaks of fantasy and ecstasy in a post-Freudian generation, the first thing that usually comes to mind is sexual ecstasy.

We therefore come to it last. No doubt sex, and the relations between the sexes, and all the tensions and awkwardnesses generated by this dimension of our being are frequent themes in joking, clowning, and comedy. And there are those enterprising Freudians, beginning with Freud himself in his *Wit and the Unconscious* and especially *Totem and Taboo*, who have dreamed of crediting most of humor and most of religion and even most of human culture to the surplus of this account.

Not even Ferdinand the bull is safe from sexualist interpretation. According to one Freudian analyst, Ferdinand is a pre-Oedipal and narcissistic figure who is refusing to grow up and enter the Oedipal world. The soft corks on his favorite tree represent the limp phallus of boyhood. The flowers are his attachment to mother. His disinterest in preparing for the bullring is his unwillingness to rebel against, castrate, and kill the father. The sting of the bumblebee is an external attempt at awakening sexual desire and an aggressive will-to-power. But when the sting wears off, he is still not interested in murdering father-figures (the bullfighter and picadors) or raping mother-substitutes (the beautiful ladies in the stands). So he is taken home in disgrace, still infantile, sexually impotent, socially powerless, and in effect castrated.[15]

For those with smaller Freudian enthusiasms, such ready-made categories of interpretation may seem as humorous as the fact that King Oedipus himself had no desire to kill his father or wed his mother. But even in Freudian terms, what is missed is the trans-Oedipal and post-Oedipal character of the symbolism. Ferdinand has a secret, and this secret is not narcissism, attachment to the mother, castration, or regression. It has something to do with going beyond the Freudian Oedipus and the Sophoclean Oedipus. It has to do with the nature of maturity.

When one is disposed, for whatever reasons, to approach even so simple a defense of simplicity as *The Story of Ferdinand* in the ominous terms of murder and rape——or, failing these, the choice of infantilism and regression to the womb——it is time to bring forth the Greek god Comus, from whose name the term comedy probably derives. In the first place, Comus was not one of the great gods who played a major dramatic role in Greek mythology, and that in itself is symbolically significant. He was not party to the bloody power-struggles, the court intrigue, the sexual exploits, or the titanic conflicts of these gods and goddesses. While he *was* a fertility god, he was not such in the grand manner of Dionysus or the goddess Aphrodite, let alone in the sense of representing Oedipal jealousy of the father and desire for the mother. He was not noted for or supportive of excess, whether in the realm of power, sex, or family.

Comus was the god of fertility in that relatively unexciting, intramarital, down-on-the-farm, barnyard sense. He was not a god of heady wine, fantastic sexual exploits, and inflamed passions. His province was that of the basic, around-home concerns of life: sexual companionship, begetting children, family welfare, productive fields, and healthy animals. As a god of fertility, Comus was inevitably like Dionysus in some respects, and was also represented by a phallus. But his sex was something normal and ordinary and essential to survival, not something abnormal or frenzied or orgiastic. As Joseph Meeker commented,

Comus was content to leave matters of great intellectual import to Apollo and gigantic passions to Dionysus while he busied himself with the maintenance of the commonplace conditions that are friendly to life. Maintaining equilibrium among living things, and restoring it once it has been lost, are Comus's special talents, and they are shared by the many comic heroes who follow the god's example.[16]

While Greek comedy has its origin in the Dionysian festival, it shows itself even in its Dionysian context, and dedicated to Dionysus, as belonging to Comus, for even in the act of giving vent to revelry and license, comedy does so, after all, comically. Comedy is concerned with relieving and moderating tensions, not supercharging them. This principle we continue to follow even today in film comedies, by making exceptionally beautiful and sexy blondes dumb, or desired by blundering males. Any of the extreme physical displays of comedy are simultaneously a matter of joke and parody. When "country boy" in an old Japanese print comes into town to show everyone how it is really done, he comes with a penis so gigantic that it requires a procession of several wagons to carry it. That is the comic perception of excess and ecstasy.

Both Aristophanes and Kratinos "honored" Dionysus in their comedies by portraying him as a bit of a fool, with a penchant for getting into uncomfortable and humiliating situations—as sex, and passion, generally, seem to have a tendency to do. The ribald humor and phallic exhibition in the performances of their plays had the same import. Sex can be rather awkward and complicating. And since the phallus was so conspicuously depicted as a Dionysian symbol and generously displayed at his festival, humor was invited and needed. All the Athenian colonies, furthermore, were required to send phalli in special procession to his festival. And if one can imagine the scene of a crowd parading a large phallus to Athens, one can readily see how a theatrical comedy might have developed from the "revel songs" and witticisms of those who carried the phalli in procession!

If one turns from Dionysus to Apollo and his dedication to law and order, rationality and principle, one finds the same result, only in reverse. When the husbands in Aristophanes' *Lysistrata* go off to war, sacrificing normal family life for patriotic ideals, distant causes, and intangible virtues, the women are outraged. Led by Lysistrata, they go on strike and deliver an ultimatum of their own to both sides for unconditional surrender. No more sexual favors will be forthcoming unless the men abandon their flag-waving and heroic talk and foolish fighting and return to bed. "Make love not war" wins the day. The men of both sides go home, and life returns to the undramatic mundanities of job, wife, children, neighbors, and housekeeping.

The picture that emerges from ancient comedy is one of moderating all the excesses and tragic impasses to which figures like Apollo and Dionysus are susceptible: reason and passion, order and abandon, sublime heights and subliminal depths. The extremes of such polarities are parodied as opposite forms of folly. And they are brought under the rule of the small kingdom of Comus, where the most lofty and most profound values are the ordinary ones. It is the kingdom of cork trees and water buckets and hungry kids, of sand castles and triangular shoes and plain beans, of bees and minnows and the lice of elephants. It is the kingdom of nothing special.

David Miller has suggested that, as in ancient Greece, "there are two paths in our time, alternative mythologies for a period of crisis: *up and out* (the rational, heroic, masculine way) and *down and in* (the mad, mystical, feminine way)."[17] And as a report on the fantasies and ecstasies of the day, this is certainly correct. It can hardly be disputed that the *extra*ordinary, in whatever form, is the great preoccupation of our time. We have been spirited away by high-flying birds and low-flying pornography, ideological fervor and occult powers, nationalistic loyalties and charismatic intoxication. We have been accosted by drug peddlers, sorcerers' apprentices, demons needing an exorcist, witchcraft revivals, flying ghosts and flying saucers, chariots from the gods, and other visitants from outer space. We have been spurred on by dreams of greatness and number-oneness, new frontiers, new worlds to conquer, and all the sundry ladders of success, while visions of superheroes, superstars, supersalespeople, and supersex have danced before us.

But the truly heroic person in our midst is no longer the hero. We have been bombarded by the most incredible variety of heroes and counterheroes imaginable. We have been stampeded back and forth between the "up and out" and the "down and in," as if herded into the to-and-fro of an accelerated Hegelian dialectic. The real hero of our time is the common person, the cipher in the faceless mass, who may be buffeted and bewildered and often caught in the struggle between Eagles and Serpents, but who somehow through it all manages to remain relatively sane, simple, ordinary, and human. Our hero is the nonhero, like Ferdinand the bull, who is content to sit under his cork tree and sniff flowers. And though he may be stimulated to the most heroic displays and frenzied abandon by the sting of some bumblebee, he will return to the simple wonder of sniffing daisies under his marvelous tree.

The truth is that the Apollonian passion for order and perfection, as well as the boisterous abandon of Dionysus, are the forms of our *ecstasis*, not just the wild, mad, irrational surfacings of subterranean excess. The elaboration of ritual and the intricacies of ceremonial pomp, the compulsion of the meticulous person, the relentless drive for possession, the ambition of comprehending or conquering the world, the restless quest for progress and improvement, the perennial fabrication of new utopias—all this is also *ecstasis*, and the excess of constantly exceeding and succeeding. It is the *ecstasis* and excess of the "up and out."

This is not to dismiss either form of ecstasy. We need our visions, our hopes, our grand imaginings, our impossible dreams, our revelries, and our moments of escape. These are a part of both the greatness and the foolishness of our existence. But their function is not simply to carry us outside ourselves, and in that act to devalue or empty the present moment and our common life of its intrinsic power and mystery. It is to revitalize and revalue the here and now. We stand outside in order to stand more profoundly and deeply within. Even heroes must spend most of their time, like the rest of us, in that valley that lies between mountain heights and ocean depths. The essential human problem is to come to terms with that valley, its own marvels and miracles, not just to invent more and more ingenious methods of escape.

Above may be the Apollonian heights, and below the Dionysian deeps. And there we wander now and then in our fantasies, our festivities, and our folly. But our real home, and the true center of our being, is not to be found in either place. It is here, now, everywhere before us at all times.

. . . We shall not cease from exploration
And the end of all our exploring
Will be to arrive where we started
And know the place for the first time.
Through the unknown, remembered gate
When the last of earth left to discover
Is that which was the beginning;
At the source of the longest river
The voice of the hidden waterfall
And the children in the apple-tree
Not known, because not looked for
But heard, half-heard, in the stillness
Between two waves of the sea.
Quick now, here, now, always—
A condition of complete simplicity. . . .[18]

Chapter 7

Tragic Castles
and Comic Cottages

In much wisdom is much vexation,
and [one] who increases knowledge
increases sorrow.

—Ecclesiastes 1:18

According to a medieval collection of tales, King Solomon was once visited by a wandering fool from the east named Marcolf. A series of confrontations ensued between the celebrated wisdom of Solomon and what proved to be the larger wisdom of the fool. While Solomon was reputed to be the wisest person in all the kingdom, Marcolf persisted in besting him every time. He topped Solomon's proverbs or discovered some flaw in them. He solved his toughest riddles or posed riddles that even Solomon could not solve. He confounded his authority by playing various pranks and tricks that ran rings around the less agile official wisdom. Marcolf represented a kind of basic, common-sense, practical wisdom, along with a healthy amount of shrewdness, cunning, and what more recently has come to be called "Yankee ingenuity."

As one might expect, after a time the royal dignity and patience wore thin, and Solomon commanded that the fool be hanged. When Marcolf appeared before the king, however, he asked if it were not fitting that he at least be granted one dying request. Solomon in all his wisdom acknowledged the justice of the request and granted him one final wish. Marcolf then said, "O king, my desire is that I may be able to choose the tree from which I am to be hanged." To Solomon this seemed fair enough, and the wish was granted. The legend then concludes: "So Marcolf and the king's soldiers travelled through the valley of Josaffat, and over the hill of Olivet, and from thence to Jericho, and over the river Jordan, and through all Arabia, and over the Grand Desert to the Red Sea, and *never* did Marcolf find the tree from which he chose to be hanged."[1]

The difference between tragic heroes and comic heroes is difficult to define, but one suspects it has something to do with hanging. From King Oedipus to King Lear, tragic heroism has had a penchant for defining the tree from which it might be hung. In the name of freedom it often builds its own prison house. In the name of knowledge it increases sorrow and vexation. In the name of power it multiplies the forms of bondage. In the name of courage and *conviction* it often pushes recklessly ahead without regard for consequences. In the name of duty and loyalty, honor or prestige, God and country, it often sacrifices the very people involved on the altar of principle and virtue. In the name of divine revelations or a dedication to truth, sacred creeds or righteous causes, it often turns its salvations into Pyrrhic victories or unredeemable damnations. In the name of transcending human circumstances it often results in opening up new abysses for itself and others.

The warning comes from Greek tragedy itself:

Unwise are those who aspire,
Aiming to go beyond the limits of humanity. . . . .
He that seeks glory, he who pursues
Some unbounded, superhuman dream,
May lose the harvest that he has,
And reap death instead.[2]

While tragic freedom has a habit of getting itself chained like Prometheus or blinded like Oedipus, comic freedom offers a liberation and transcendence of its own in the midst of limitation. There is no tree from which it chooses to be hung.

The tragic problem is not so much one of necessity or fate, militating against human freedom, but one of a loss of perspective and balance, as the tragedies themselves would often remind their audiences. Freedom, tragically conceived, for all its nobility and promise of glory, so easily becomes its own undoing. Freedom is a precarious blessing, as are all the other capacities and virtues that tragedy extols: courage, loyalty, duty, pride, power, authority, determination, conviction, justice, aspiration, perfection. Whenever such virtues lose their flexibility and their concrete humanity, and freedom locks itself into an unvariable commitment, tragic freedom becomes tragic inevitability.

All the noblest ideals of tragic inspiration so easily turn into something less than, or even opposite, their intention. This is the irony that Sophoclean tragedies like *Oedipus Rex* and *Antigone* explored in masterful torment very early in the genre. A tenacious clinging to principles and virtues, however admirable, lead unavoidably to stifling and destructive consequences. Hence the necessity for the tragic vision to be tempered and "humanized" by the comic vision. If there is a "tragic flaw," it lies at least in part in the absence of the comic spirit and perspective. How many are the trees from which we propose to hang ourselves!

Comic heroes, like Marcolf, are thus exemplars of a special human freedom and flexibility—which, after all, is the real genius of the race. Naked as we are, and bereft of physical endowments comparable to the higher animal orders, the secret of human survival over the past million years or so is that we are adaptable. We are endowed with a brain that—along with the capacity for imagining all sorts of paradises and utopias for ourselves, and an equal number of holocausts and hells for our enemies—is capable of imagining an endless variety of alternative modes of being, believing, and doing. We are not locked into an unvarying set of biologically imprinted behavioral patterns. Instead, we have developed an unending variety of cultural substitute-forms. While these substitute-forms can in turn become as rigid as a biological imprint, and thus violate the very freedom that gave them birth, it has been the task of clowns and fools and comic heroes to remind us of our intrinsic freedom and flexibility.

Unlike the rest of the animal kingdom, and more like the ancient trickster and shapeshifter, we are not easily pinned down and defined, whether in our nature or our behavior or our symbolic repertoire. We are tricky little devils. To be sure, our unpredictability and amorphousness can at times be threatening to a sense of our own clear and solid identity or to a simple belief in a common humanity. Yet it makes possible our peculiar capacity for survival under the most difficult and diverse circumstances. We have lived in caves and palaces, deserts and fertile valleys, igloos and tropical huts, monasteries and harems. We have been patriarchal and matriarchal, monarchists and anarchists, capitalists and communists. We have been animists and polytheists and monotheists and atheists and even presbyterians. And we have survived.

This flexibility and freedom has another side, which is also taken into the province of comedy. By virtue of having a mental capacity well in excess of what is normally needed for survival, humans have to have something to do, if it is only a matter of *decorating* this survival. To be sure, we are inclined to speak of the matter in more lofty terms, such as creativity, imagination, reason, spirit, perhaps "divine image and likeness." But it is this cerebral "having to have something to do" that opens up the whole range of human culture, and specifically human preoccupation. We organize not only pastime activities like sports and entertainment, but also art, craft, education, science, politics, and even myth and ritual. We *play* with our existence. Having satisfied the barest necessities, we invent new "necessities," more and more intricate and elaborate games with which to occupy our time, engage our minds, keep our hands busy, flatter our fragile self-consciousness, and give meaning and direction to our lives.

Animals have enough brainpower to get by and get the job of survival done, given their ecological niches. But humans have such a considerable surplus to play with that one of the most basic problems is that of boredom. Mentally we are like the small child who must constantly be squirming, wiggling, jumping, singing, dancing, chattering, and in general producing astounding amounts of noise and confusion for its size. We are not satisfied simply to tear off chunks of the carcasses of gazelles and then lie in the sun or shade until the pangs of hunger begin to stir us again. Whether primitive or modern hunter, we feel compelled to surround our hunting with all sorts of myths and rituals, customs and meanings. We must decorate the hunters, decorate the weapons, decorate the meat, decorate the eating place, and decorate the trophy, or decorate with it. We must cook the kill, and in a certain way. We must eat it in a certain manner, with certain instruments, at certain times, in certain places, with certain people, supplemented by certain other foods, consumed in certain orders and combinations, and accompanied by certain kinds of conversation, dress, furniture, music, lighting, and prayers.

Even the simple requirement of eating for survival is turned into an elaborate aesthetic, ethical, social, and religious game, with rules and styles and mannerisms as varied as the variety of human cultures. None of this has anything directly to do with the physiology of digestion and absorption. And, to compound the issue, after we have eaten we consider ourselves to have replenished our energy for all sorts of *other* activities, most of which also have little to do with the basic necessities of life and survival.

This superabundance of mental energy, under whatever name, is our Promethean/Adamic nature. It is the source of our flexibility and adaptability and freedom. But it may also be turned into the source of our inflexibility and bondage. When the games that we have developed and play become absolutized in a rigidity of forms and dogmatized in an inerrant justification of those forms—like insisting that there is only one right way to play poker—we destroy the very imagination and playfulness and freedom that made possible those enrichments of human existence. Human beings seem to have the peculiar habit of organizing the most ingenious cultural games and then throwing themselves into those games with a singleness of purpose and passionate involvement that quite forgets the game and the playfulness. The new vistas that have been opened up by our capacity for playing with our existence are closed off again and sealed in seriousness and the need for security. This forgetfulness and closing and sealing is at the root of tragic conflict and is the tragic contradiction of a freedom that issues in bondage and death.

In literary terms, the themes of comic freedom, adaptability, and survival are the special emphasis of the picaresque hero, like the sixteenth-century Lazarillo de Tormes or Grimmelshausen's seventeenth-century *Simplicius Simplicissimus*. The picaro is generally an ordinary citizen having no political power, wealth, or social status, a relative nobody caught in a world of competing forces or faced with a world of indifference. Lazarillo does not belong to a noble line or a prominent family or a great cause or the "mainstream of history." But like an orphaned street urchin who is wise and wily because of the necessity to do or die, Lazarillo has learned to use his intelligence to survive, to remain free of spirit, and to maintain a kind of rugged, self-reliant identity.

The picaro is not an idealist—in fact, the picaro is a bit of a rogue (*picaro*) with an irrepressible sense of life as a game. For the picaro, the real problem is how to keep from being trampled by or enlisted in the fray of conflicting powers (whether religious creeds, political ambitions, or national loyalties). Simplicius comes forth out of the insane carnage of Protestant/Catholic Europe during the Thirty Years' War. His own village is in ruins, and "Christian" civilization is in apparent ruins. But he comes with a determination to make his own way, and with the droll observation that "this introductory entertainment almost spoiled my desire to see the world."

Among the English, the number-one rogue is Shakespeare's Sir John Falstaff, that "huge bombard of sack" who moves so merrily outside the conventional honesties and dishonesties of his time with a great love of wine and life and laughter. He is a bit of a rascal and a ruffian, but that is not because of some streak of meanness in him. Rather, it is because he has such a zest for living that human orders and human ideals are always getting in the way. Whereas others may put their lives in the enlisted service of some cause or ambition, Sir John is primarily enthusiastic about life itself. His largeness of heart and frame and his raucous laughter would embrace all in a common contagion.

Tragic heroes—at least from Sophocles on—so easily destroy themselves and others. They crush and are crushed by their own stubborn idealism and vain pride. They take the game, whatever the game, so seriously and uncompromisingly. And though tragic heroes may die in a blaze of glory or a final shout of defiance, or be awarded some posthumous vindication, comic heroes live on in their playful, middling-muddling manner. They imagine a considerable variety of options between being "red or dead."

Flexibility is, after all, the characteristic of life; rigidity is the sign of death. Flexibility is even the secret of airplane wings and skyscraper technology. Because comic heroes do not lose themselves in absolute seriousness, rigid principles, and unwavering pursuit, they are better adapted for survival—theirs, and those who are associated with them, and even those who are opposed to them. Because they do not refuse to walk anything but a straight line, do not insist on barricading themselves within unchangeable systems, do not always believe their own rhetoric, they are not easily trapped. They wrestle with life, to be sure, and rather valiantly. But they wrestle like greased pigs. As Hegel observed:

In tragedy individuals are thrown into confusion in virtue of the abstract nature of their sterling volition and character. . . . What on the other hand is inseparable from the comic is an infinite geniality and confidence capable of rising superior to its own contradiction, and experiencing therein no taint of bitterness or sense of misfortune whatever.[3]

Some comic heroes, however, *are* hanged. The freedom and flexibility of the comic vision—if too threatening to the powers that be—may result in crucifixion or burning at the stake. Clowns and fools, at least symbolically, have often suffered for their license by being flogged or driven from the ritual arena. The liberty available to jesters to parody the king and to dance outside the protocol of the court always involved the risk of being beheaded for their pains. Comic iconoclasm in particular may offer the dual reward of freedom and imprisonment. The redheaded McMurphy, in Kesey's *One Flew over the Cuckoo's Nest*, swaggers into the asylum to which he has been committed with a laugh so free and loud that it reverberates through the hollow halls, and with a determination to teach fellow inmates how to loosen up and live a little. But he runs squarely into Big Nurse, whose therapeutic ordering has all but suffocated the last breath of self-respecting humanity in her charges and reduced them to the numbed submission of automatons. Though the "gambling fool" teaches the "loonies" to play once more and to laugh with something more than nervous, squeaky bird chirps, he is eventually sent up for shock treatments and finally for a frontal lobotomy. Still he is the victor in the end, for through him others have been set free.

And You Shall Be as Gods

From the lofty standpoint of tragedy or any drama of high seriousness, comedy and the comic hero no doubt appear as pale and shifting seconds, on the order of moonlight to solar radiance. Certainly a formidable array of literary scholars have insisted that comedy comes after tragedy, after the sublime, after the ideal. Tragedy therefore presents itself as more fundamental and profound than comedy, the real substance of which comedy is the mock reflection—or, as James Thurber put it, "the tragic is the robust wine, the dramatic the champagne of the arts, while comedy is the gingerale."

But a partisan of comedy could just as well argue the contrary. Human beings share seriousness with the animals, but in laughter they laugh alone—or to a preliminary extent with the chimpanzee. The comic sense goes beyond taking things "straight" and univocally, in that remarkable human capacity for seeing words and situations in double and even multiple senses. Tragic heroism has a Promethean/Oedipal air of adolescence about it. Comic heroism, with its flexibility and inclination to compromise, its playfulness and delight in ambiguity, its knowing winks and lighter countenance, is the more mature form. If comedy comes after tragedy—as in the Dionysian performances where the tragic trilogy was followed by an irreverent satyr play and a comedy—it comes as a reaffirmation of those aspects of the human condition which tragedy has neglected, and therefore as the larger perspective and fuller spirit. Jonathan Swift stated it boldly: "In Comedy the best actor plays the part of the droll, while some second rogue is made the hero or fine gentleman. So, in this farce of life, wise men pass their time in mirth, while fools are only serious."

To attempt a comparison between tragedy and comedy for the purpose of declaring which is superior and more profound is not a very helpful exercise. We would do well at most to come with Christopher Fry "to the verge of saying that comedy is greater than tragedy"—or any other dramatic form. Even in the Dionysian theater, a comedy was placed in competition not with a tragedy but with other comic entries. Shakespeare wrote both great tragedies and great comedies, suggesting not only that it can be done, but that the two genres serve different purposes, have different goals, aim at different effects. Comparing them in order to assign a prize or affix a seal is like comparing essays and poems, which at best could only be the registry of a personal taste.

Tragedy, as Aristotle observed, aims at human greatness, the noble and honorable and sublime. And if in tragedy the praises of humanity are sung, it is clearly a heroic humanity, exceptional individuals and their exceptional acts who, even when they sin, sin in a grand manner.

Comedy is more modest and magnanimous. It is in comedy that humanity is celebrated and enjoyed and laughed over, more or less as it is. If there are comic sins, they tend to be on the order of pranks and tricks. Comic crimes are petty crimes, deserved crimes, crimes that backfire or are of doubtful result. Perhaps they are crimes that are wildly successful, then abysmal failures because of the most trivial omission—like being apprehended for failing to put a nickel in the parking meter next to the getaway car.

When one speaks of praise-singing relative to human enterprises, however, one senses that we are in the world of rhetoric, rhapsody, eulogy—the world of commencement speeches, political conventions, national holidays, funeral orations, corporation meetings, and paid commercials. "Numberless are the world's wonders," sings the chorus of *Antigone*, "but none more wonderful than man." Then recounted, as in the *Prometheus Bound* of Aeschylus, are all the marvels of human achievement. Carefully omitted, of course, are a number of other, less glorious marvels. Or, when they are included, and the conflict and irony begins to build, we move toward tragedy in the darker sense. Even Hamlet, in the midst of the monumental miseries and injustices he suffers and sees strewn about him, clings tenaciously to the heroic vision of the species:

What a piece of work is a man! How noble in reason! How infinite in faculty! In form and moving, how express and admirable! In action how like an angel! In apprehension, how like a god! The beauty of the world! The paragon of animals!

—*Hamlet*, Act 2, Scene 2

Tragedy is selective in what it chooses to admire about human nature and accomplishment. And it is just this tension between eulogy and actuality, its incredible irony, and frequently its darkly tragic consequences as well, that comedy immediately notices and puts on display. In comedy, after listening to hymns of praise for the species, one has the choice of either gagging, throwing up, or laughing. The comic impulse being what it is, comedy counters with any of several devices. It may exaggerate the praise and its object even further—though in some cases this seems hardly possible. It may exaggerate the act and gestures of praising, depicting as infinitely praiseworthy some creature that is anything but, like a eulogy of a mule. Or it may confront head-on the contradiction between the panegyrics and the circumstances. As W.C. Fields put it in *Tillie and Gus* (1933), "There comes a time in the affairs of man when he must take the bull by the tail, and squarely face the situation!"

For Hegel, "the true theme of primitive tragedy is the godlike." And whereas tragedy exemplifies "the godlike manifestations of the human heart," comic figures "make visible the general perversity of mankind" (*Philosophy of Fine Art*). While there is some truth in the distinction, its terms are quite ambiguous. And that ambiguity comedy goes out of its way to detail, to play with, and to enjoy. A part of what comedy makes "visible" is this very aspiration or claim to godlikeness itself, and the perversities to which even the most well-meaning heroism and nobly heroic virtues are subject. This is its prophetic-iconoclastic function. Comedy shares in something of the same insight that led the Yahwist to credit the promise "You shall be like God" to a serpent-tempter.

Adolf Hitler, after all, had lofty aspirations for uniting Europe, vindicating a humiliated Germany, reestablishing strong leadership, breaking down class and economic bonds, and revitalizing old Germanic values. He came as a savior (*Führer*) of his people and of Western civilization, bringing a new enthusiasm and promise and hope. And he evoked a deep sense of loyalty and commitment, self-sacrifice, and exalted destiny. Yet in these grandiose visions and god-playings, as well as the various personal and ideological idiosyncrasies that accompanied this godlikeness, Hitler was also a perverse fool among fools. As such he was appropriately depicted in Chaplin's comedy *The Great Dictator*, and especially Bertolt Brecht's tragicomedy *The Rise and Fall of Arturo Ui*. The tragedy of Hitler and of the world that came tumbling down with him had much to do with the prior lack of any refined comic sensibility relative to such "godlike manifestations of the human heart." Godlikeness is a self-image that we have played with for a good part of our history, in one form or another. In real life the comic awareness that Chaplin and Brecht portrayed has been woefully tragic in its absence.

"You shall be like God"—how much human energy has been expended in working on that fantasy or being destroyed by it or bemoaning its unattainability. For Plato the supreme goal was "to become like God, as far as this is possible for a mortal" (*Republic* 10.613a-b). For Pindar, though humans have a kinship with the gods—by virtue of the belief that "from one mother both came forth,"—humans have received, as it were, the short end of the stick. "The powers have been so divided that the one is as nothing, while the other is securely established in the eternal heavens" (*Nemean* 6:1). Thus in reason, imagination, creativity, and foresight, humans have certain affinities with the gods. But those powers are very limited and partial, are mixed with mortal flesh, and are often the source of their own undoing. Epimetheus (afterthought) is the brother of Prometheus (forethought).

Nowhere is this problem more painfully rehearsed than among the Greek heroes, for the hero is the superlative instance of human strength, beauty, and intellect. How like the gods! And yet how quickly the youthful flower of vigor and virtue fades! How suddenly the mighty hero is slain in battle and becomes a rotting corpse! How overnight the labor of years is reduced to rubble! The dramatic effect of this pathos is further heightened by mythologically accounting for the splendor of the hero by crediting the hero's birth to a mixed divine/human marriage. This was no ordinary human, but a god-man. Yet in the end, as with the heel of Achilles, the hero too proves vulnerable and mortal. No matter how close to divinity, no matter how carefully drawn the hero's plans and how relentless the hero's struggles, still, like the hair shorn from Samson in his weakness for Delilah, the human element eventually brings life and dreams crashing down upon the hero and those around.

Out of this vision of human existence comes a sense of tragic conflict between human realities and divine aspirations, mortal flesh and dreams of immortality, finite limitations and infinite imaginings. But the same conflicts are also the source of comedy. If tragedy deals with oppositions, tensions between contrarieties, worlds in collision, so does comedy, though more in the manner with which the queen in *Alice in Wonderland* disposes of them. When the queen orders the cheshire cat beheaded, the executioner makes bold to suggest, "You can't cut off a head unless there is a body to cut it off from," while the queen insists, "If something isn't done about it in less than no time, I'll have everybody beheaded!"

The comic hero—like the trickster, clown, and fool—incarnates the essential ambiguity of our natures and the awkwardness and bewilderment of being human. Basic to these many forms is the same thesis—comically understood—that we are creatures of very diverse and often opposite tendencies. We are suspended, as it were, between heaven and earth, eternity and time, the infinite and the finite, spirit and flesh, rationality and impulse, altruism and selfishness, pride and insecurity. We are compounded of sunlight and stone, intelligence and ignorance, the divine image and the dust of the earth, the cleverness of Prometheus and the foolishness of Epimetheus. And if there is any "salvation" forthcoming, it comes in the candid—rather than candid—acceptance, and even enjoyment, of this ambiguousness.

We prefer, of course, to flatter ourselves with images of idealized heroes, or at least tragic ones. And there is a certain inspiration and catharsis to be had from their heroism. Yet it has always been the task of comic heroes to identify our pretensions and self-deceptions, our inconsistencies and incongruities, if need be by exemplifying them. In their antics and adventures, their fancies and follies, we are gently reminded that, despite all the grandeur of our dreams and accomplishments, we are finite, fallible, mortal, and frequently foolish creatures of the earth. Even when our heads are in the clouds, our feet walk on the ground and are made of clay.

For the comic protagonist, life is never so simple, so sensible, so logical, and so arranged as our inspirational visions, our theatrical plots, our historical reconstructions, or our great works of art might wish to suggest. There everything may be neatly arranged, sorted out, pieced together, all wrapped up, as so many tightly woven stories with a beginning, a progression, a climax, and an end—or as so many paintings with a theme and structure and composition, forming an ordered whole, finished and complete. The comic artist knows life to be otherwise and people to be otherwise. The world is seen, as Pirandello put it, "if not exactly in the nude, then as, so to speak, in its shirt-tails. It is in his shirt-tails that he sees the king, who makes such a fine impression on you when you see him 'composed' in the majesty of enthronement, with his crown and sceptre and mantle of purple and ermine."[4] In the latter form the king is a composition, an appearance, an illusion of reality. Actually such a king, like such a hero or such a world, does not exist.

Hence comes, in the art of humor, all that seeking after more minute and intimate details, even details that may appear trivial and vulgar when set alongside the idealized syntheses of art in general; hence that seeking after the contrasts and contradictions on which the humorist's art is based, as opposed to the consistency sought by others; and hence all that breaking down, that unraveling, that whimsicality, all those digressions that mark the work of the humorist, as opposed to the ordered piecing together, the "composed" nature, of works of art.[5]

The result, however, is not simply a breaking down, an unraveling. It is a putting together of a different sort: the silly is mixed in with the sublime, the simple with the sophisticated, the miscellaneous with the monumental, because that is the way the totality of the picture, the whole of life, really is. Out of the comic "composition" an odd sort of wholeness and unity results, a kind of *coincidence of opposites* without entirely losing the opposition. In such comic realism, human limitations and aspirations, follies and successes, are gracefully welcomed in all their awkwardness.

Here, paradoxically, comedy approaches its own form of heroic greatness relative to which even the tragic catharsis is the simpler and easier way out. One approaches, and quite unprepossessingly, the very sphere of the divine, the transcendent laughter of the gods. For comedy, in the course of being frankly human and refusing to be trapped by its own human aspirations and conflicts, has something of the divine—the truly cosmic—perspective in it. It proceeds from a higher and larger vantage point in which molehills are not confused with mountains, people do not loom as large as gods, and the greatest deeds for good or ill are but ripples on a single wave in a limitless cosmic sea.

On the one hand, comedy laughs from a position that is totally *within* the human condition, for it accepts that condition and sees itself as a part of that condition, even offering itself as the vehicle for laughter. Yet in the act of espousing and identifying with the human condition, comedy expresses its peculiar freedom. At the same time, it views the human condition from *beyond* itself, as it were, *sub specie aeternitatis*. In both senses comedy has a capacity to ameliorate and reconcile and redeem what the tragic hero cannot. In Enid Welsford's words,

The serious hero focuses events, forces issues, and causes catastrophes; but the Fool by his mere presence dissolves events, evades issues, and throws doubt on the finality of fact.

The Stage-clown therefore is as naturally detached from the play as the Court-fool is detached from social life. And the fool's most fitting place in literature is as hero of the episodic narrative, or as the voice speaking from without and not from within the dramatic plot. . . . The fool is a creator, not of beauty but of spiritual freedom. The fool is an emancipator.[6]

Tragic Wars and Comic Games

The dramatic presuppositions and controlling metaphors of heroic/tragic literatures are, after all, very much the legacy of warrior cultures and the warrior ethos. Existence is conceived in the images of the battleground. All things are sorted out into opposing forces arrayed against one another: light and darkness, life and death, cosmos and chaos. The element of struggle in all life for survival is abstracted and amplified as the central key to reality. And this key is further understood in terms of that peculiarly human form of struggle, war. Thus the divine and the human, higher and lower natures, old and new orders, family and state, parent and child, civilized and savage—all are basically in conflict with one another. These antagonistic and often violent relationships, in turn, provide the dramatic plot. Drama is the narration of conflict, as history is the record of triumphs and defeats.

For several millennia this stirring image of heroes and their battle cries and their bloody battles has dominated the great civilizations, and religious literature as well. The martial scenario of Greek gods and heroes is but one instance among many. The Babylonian god of order, Marduk, is perennially beseiged by Tiamat, goddess of watery chaos. The Canaanite fertility god, Baal, is annually slain and dismembered by Mot, god of death and desolation. The Hebraic "Lord of Hosts," "mighty in battle," destroys the enemies of Israel, smashes "high places" and other "abominations," and commands the genocide of all conquered peoples. The Zoroastrian god of light (Ahura Mazda) is at war throughout history with the spirit of darkness (Angra Mainyu), and blessed are they who choose to fight on the side of light. A Christian mythology appropriates the same cosmic conflict between God and Satan, angels and demons, heaven and hell, culminating in a final battle of Armageddon. Muslims actively enlist in the cause through *jihad* (holy war), crushing idolatry and idolaters in the name of Allah. In Asia the Aryan war-god Indra, recipient of more hymns than any other divinity in the *Rig-veda*, is hailed as the powerful "destroyer of fortresses" and "slayer of the foe"—the defeated Indus peoples. The beloved *Bhagavad-gita* has as its setting the war chariots and bloodbaths of the Indian *Mahabharata*. The great mother-goddesses of India, Kali and Durga, are depicted with necklaces of skulls, girdles of severed arms, swords in hand, lapping from bowls the blood that gushes from the heads of decapitated victims. Even a quietistic Zen Buddhism becomes heavily involved with the martial arts and the samurai class.

A seemingly endless list of examples could be produced from the religions of the world, so deeply and almost universally has this vision "captured" the human imagination. Whether the commandment has been to "utterly destroy" every Hittite, Amorite, Canaanite, Perizzite, Hivite and Jebusite—man, woman, child, infant, and beast (Deut. 20:17) or to "put on the whole armor of God [Eph. 6:11]" and "fight the good fight of the faith [1 Tim. 6:12]," the dominant images and metaphors through which life is to be perceived and lived are those of warfare and conquest.

In varying combinations, corresponding warrior virtues have also been extolled, from Homer's *Iliad* to Nietzsche's *Zarathustra* and Kierkegaard's *Training in Christianity*: strength, courage, conviction, loyalty, duty, honor, unyielding dedication, indomitable will, passionate involvement, uncompromising determination. Pagan, Christian, and anti-Christian alike have stirred to the rallying cry of such virtues as these. And how quickly and easily the more spiritualized reinterpretation of the old warrior ethic and world view slips back into a literal and political application. The knight and the "knight of faith" become practically indistinguishable.

To some extent the comic hero, unlike the comic nonhero, shares in this "Sturm und Drang" mythology, for there is surely something admirable and uplifting and rousing about these warrior virtues. And there is an obvious historical reality to conflicting principles and forces—much of it in fulfillment of such a world view itself. But the comic hero enlists in the army, if enlisting at all, as one come to introduce a certain amount of confusion in the ranks and chaos on the battlefield. In the presence of such a figure, distinctions between friend and foe, the righteous and the unrighteous, generals and privates, tend to become fuzzy and ill-fitting. The comic soldier does not quite fit in, even when making a valiant effort to do so. Whether in the officers' quarters or the supply depot or on the front line, the comic soldier comes bringing a combination of cleverness and ineptness that tends to collapse the military hierarchy, and cancel out the effectiveness of both sides in the conflict. Such soldiering is frequently out of step and seems privy to a different set of signals.

Comic heroism does not manifest a reckless determination to die in one's boots, weapon in hand, with a look of defiance stamped on one's face. It seems more inclined to the view that "they that take up the sword shall die by the sword." Other things may well be taken up instead, as Laurel and Hardy and the Three Stooges and the Marx Brothers were particularly noted for doing: hammers, pitchforks, broom handles, china vases, hat pins, squirt guns, flowerpots, itching powders, and the like. While the comic intent may not always wear the halo of turning swords into plowshares and spears into pruning hooks, the result is at least that of dulling or misplacing swords and turning spears into fishing poles.

The drift of comic flights is that of nobody getting seriously hurt. A considerable amount of cleanup may be necessary following the battle, but there is a distinct preference for replacing lethal missiles with mudballs and spitballs and gooey cream pies. As in the many postwar comedies that dealt in a farcical manner with war—*Sergeant Bilko, At War with the Army, McHale's Navy, Hogan's Heroes, Gomer Pyle, M.A.S.H.*—the conflict is transformed into a sport, a rivalry, perhaps a schoolyard fracas. Conflicts are returned, as it were, to that time before humans picked up even sticks and stones, a time of shouts and growls and raw strength. Fighting is redirected toward that pretechnological level of bluffs and fisticuffs, where human power is rarely deadly and not so grossly out of proportion to the need to vent anger, defend territory, obtain food, or protect home and family.

Even when the comic setting is that of the most advanced technology, disputes are usually settled in the most natural and least damaging manner. Thus in the recent Batman farces, despite the fact that the "dynamic duo" had access to the most sophisticated computerized equipment, its use was restricted to detection and apprehension. The forces of evil—Joker, Penguin, Iceman, and company—were almost invariably vanquished by conventional barroom brawling: Bam! Whap! Bonk! Socko!

Insofar as comic heroism participates in the ethic of the hero, it does so in a fundamentally different way. From the start it insists on adding another set of "virtues": flexibility, freedom, compromise, playfulness, frivolity, gratification of hunger and sexual urges, survival. Thus "armed" comic heroes are more inclined toward mock battles than real ones. They exhibit honest fear, cowardice, squeamishness, bewilderment, a preference for going fishing, and a special talent for running and hiding. They are masters of elusiveness. The early Keaton in *Cops* (1922) managed to escape the entire police force of New York City for half an hour by ingenious trickery and Olympic speed. Like Don Quixote, comic heroes occasionally take on a windmill or two. But they are not so eager to die, or to propose hanging-trees for themselves and others, or to consign anyone either now or in the hereafter to the flames.

The resoluteness of comic heroism is as preideological as it is pretechnological. Its commitment is to life and to the basics of life. Only secondarily is it concerned with the fine points of custom, mores, social hierarchy, political relationships, or even religious doctrines. It is far more concerned with saving skin than with saving face. And its defense is of persons more than principles, the spirit rather than the letter. "The Sabbath was made for man, not man for the Sabbath" might well serve as a comic motto. Comic heroes are therefore not disposed to prostituting individuals to bloodless ideas and ideals or to bloody pride and honor. Rhetoric, flag-waving, and fanaticism do not become them—except by way of exemplifying such in parody.

For comic heroism, existence is to be seen under a different set of metaphors and images. The various competing forces, whether of natural or human orders, are to be viewed more in terms of a *game* than a battle. Life is a *contest* more than a conflict, a *play* of forces, a *sporting* proposition, an *interplay* of opposites, a cosmic *dance*. Life is not intrinsically a quarrel or titanic confrontation, any more than nature is simply "red in tooth and claw." Life flows, as rivers flow, sometimes lazily in the summer sun, sometimes in a raging spring torrent; sometimes fertilizing, sometimes eroding; sometimes building up, sometimes destroying; but not necessarily at war with anything or anyone.

We are often deceived by our metaphors. There is an almost total inappropriateness in applying military imagery to plant and animal kingdoms, the physical order, or the universe at large. War is a specifically human phenomenon, and with great injustice is it applied outside the human sphere. Does light have a quarrel with darkness? Does the volcano seek to ravage the forest, or the earthquake to molest the land? Is the wolf at enmity with the caribou? Must the lion lie down with the lamb to usher in an era of peace? Is death the "last enemy" to be destroyed?

Life is not out to vanquish death, or death out to eliminate life. They only exist and have meaning relative to one another. Life needs death, and death needs life. They are two aspects of the same process, each requiring and interpenetrating its opposite. Otherwise the game would be over. Solitaire.

The comic-heroic venture, accordingly, is not that of conquest and victory, but of compromise and mediation. The goal is not to win a war at all cost, but to play the game of life, accepting its risks, its winnings, and its inevitable losings. While the dynamic of the hero is still there, it is a different sort of dynamic. And while there is a rhythm to the action, it is not from the beat of a war drum. It is more like the dynamic rhythm of meandering streams, springtime and autumn, the tidal ebb and flow, the waxing and waning of the moon—and in this sense, too, of light and darkness, life and death, cosmos and chaos. As in the dynamic of music, point and counterpoint, melody and countermelody, major and minor, euphony and dissonance juxtapose themselves, compete with one another, and in the tension between them form a higher unity, not a pitched battle.

Meeting, they laugh and laugh—
    The forest grove, the many fallen leaves.[7]

Are the summer leaves—as we might be inclined to phrase it—"fallen" as in battle, "felled" by the "relentless onslaught" of an "advancing march" of winter? Or is this the metaphorical trap? Meisetsu touches the heart of the comic understanding:

Butterflies
    love and follow this flower wreath—
        that on the coffin lies.[8]

Amid human grief and wailing, there is rejoicing in butterfly land!

Chapter 8

A Divine Comedy

*He [God] has scattered the proud in the
    imagination of their hearts,
he has put down the mighty from their
    thrones,
and exalted those of low degree.*
    —*Luke 1:51-52*

The art of comedy is a deeply human art. But it is also, in its own peculiar way, a divine art. The paradoxical possibility of comedy is that it may stand totally within the human condition as an *incarnation* of the genuinely human and yet stand apart from the human condition and above every human *logos* and *nomos*.

There is something of a comic transcendence in the words from the Magnificat in the Gospel of Luke that open this chapter. And though the immediate religious inclination has been to interpret such words in terms of a sober-somber drama of sin and salvation, their peculiarity is more fully appreciated in terms of the special genre of comedy. As the imagery itself might suggest, there is a remarkable affinity between the biblical tradition and the comic tradition which has too often been neglected because of an array of misgivings over drawing upon such associations. The themes of challenging the dominant orders and powers of the society, of "scattering the proud" and of the "put down" of the mighty, while elevating the lowly in their stead, are an important part of the symbolism of comedy and of the ancient repertoire of clowns and fools. In turn, these biblical themes have become an important part in the Western mythology of comedy.

A medieval Chester (England) nativity play does not miss the comic connection. When the wise men from the east come to Herod's palace in search of "the newborn king," but do not find him there, a disturbed and threatened Herod exclaims:

What the Devill shold this be!
A boy, a groome of Low Degree,
shold raigne above my Roialtie
and make me but a goose!

To be sure, the powerful sweep of Mary's words in the Magnificat suggests at first the grand images of conquest that belong to the dramatic mythology of the noble hero. We might be led to expect some righteous host come to topple the tyrant from the throne and trample oppression under foot. But considering that the words are being attributed to an unknown peasant girl in a most inconsequential village of Roman-occupied Israel, there is a certain "sweet madness" about them which belongs to the *comic* and the *nonheroic*. The juxtaposition of utterance and utterer—and the disparity between the two—has a topsy-turvy preposterousness about it. Its incredibility invites the same response that Abraham gave to the news that his aged wife, Sarah, was to bear him a son and that through him all nations would be blessed: *Isaac*, that is, "laughter."

Theologians and biblical scholars have customarily approached such episodes under the weighty rubrics of "salvation history," "drama of redemption," and the like. And by and large this *Heilsgeschichte* has been dealt with in much the same grave and ponderous style as the term itself. A certain brightness and lightness and innocent oddness is missing. That sense of marvelous absurdity and incredulous, wide-eyed wonder that attaches itself to great surprises, sudden amazements, and comic twists seems to get lost in the prosaic thickness of theological pedantry. And the resultant salvation lacks some of the very gaiety and delight, miracle and mystery, that is represented by the figure and birth of an infant. It is as if instead the prophecy of Ovid's *Metamorphosis* had come true, that in the last age children would be born with gray hair and wrinkled faces!

Furthermore, as we know too well from experience, this business of scattering the proud and putting down the mighty can become rather vengeful and vicious apart from the mellowing of the comic perspective. The overthrow of one tyranny is no guarantee that another will not take its place. The proud are easily replaced by the proud. The aristocratic elite is quickly exchanged for a capitalistic or socialistic elite. Vanquished inhumanities beget new inhumanities. But the prerequisites for entering *this* kingdom and its salvation are, we are given to understand, the very opposite of the triumphal entry of conquering heroes and victorious idealogues: childlikeness, meekness, humility, simplicity, tenderness, and compassion. It is a kingdom that one enters on the back of a burro, not on a resplendent white charger.

Out of Nazareth?

Something of the significance of these comic and nonheroic elements becomes clearer if one contrasts Christian and Buddhist nativity stories. The Buddhist nativity is classically heroic and aristocratic and richly embroidered with mythical fantasy and legendary glorification, while the Christian nativity—at least in its early biblical form—is quite ordinary by comparison, unpretentious in its simplicity, and much closer to comic-heroic and nonheroic forms.

In scriptures such as the *Buddhacarita, Lalitavistara, Mahaparinibbana*, and *Jataka*, the Buddha is depicted as being born to the "unconquerable" Sakya clan and to a life of princely luxury and advantage. His father is noted as a great king, "as powerful as [the war-god] Indra" and his mother as a pure and beautiful queen "like the goddess Shachi" (Indra's wife). Having heroically performed the marvelous deeds of five hundred previous incarnations, the Buddha had now come to his final and most glorious birth and had entered the womb of the graceful Maha Maya in the form of a white elephant.

Queen Maya, as she reclined on her royal couch, had dreamed that the guardians of the four quarters had transported her to the majestic Himalayas, bathed her in the pure waters of Lake Anotatta, and laid her on a silken bed in a golden mansion at the top of a silver mountain. There the Buddha, descending from the heavenly Grove of Gladness, transformed himself into a white elephant carrying a white lotus blossom and entered her womb through her right side. At the moment of conception, musical instruments began to play by themselves, people began to speak most kindly to one another, many miraculous healings took place, rivers ceased flowing, the fires of hell were quenched, trees and plants burst into bloom, and lotus flowers rained from the sky, covering the earth.

The queen's pregnancy was free from all distress and weariness. She was guarded by the devas of the four quarters, plus forty thousand devas from other worlds. The Buddha in her womb was so luminous that she could see him as clearly as a thread through a transparent gem. As her time drew near she desired to visit her family, and a golden litter was prepared for her. On the way she stopped to rest in a pleasure-grove, attended by her retinue of thousands of maids-in-waiting. The garden was exquisitely fragrant and heavily laden with a paradisal profusion of flowers, fruits, and nuts. And while the queen stood beneath the sheltering branches of the greatest of the Sal trees in the grove, she gave birth to a radiant son whose skin shone like lustrous gold. The child was delivered painlessly from her right side into a golden net carried by four angels. Upon birth the infant Buddha arose, walked seven paces toward the four directions, and declared, "I am supreme in all the earth. This is my final birth. No more shall there be birth for me."

The form and pageantry of the Christian nativity is strikingly different, and it is typical of the structure and import of biblical stories generally. Far from the aristocratic images of noble birth at the apex of the social pyramid, we are presented with a laborer's wife, belonging to a conquered people, from a poor village, the status of which—even among Jews—is suggested by the phrase "Can anything good come out of Nazareth?" Though the young wife is "great with child," she has had to make the laborious journey with her husband from Nazareth to Bethlehem because of a Roman decree that "all the world should be enrolled." The birth takes place unattended in an animal shed behind a crowded inn in which there was no room. The only witnesses are the animals in that shed and a small band of simple shepherds from the nearby hills. There is no cosmic tree or golden net or paradisal abundance, but straw for a bed and swaddling cloth and the smell of manure. Though later wise men from the east come to Herod's palace to pay homage to a newborn "king," they find him in the only place consistent with the rest of the biblical tradition: among the lowest of the low. And the result of their visit is that Mary and Joseph are forced to flee with the child Jesus into Egypt to escape King Herod's threatened slaughter of young male children!

While there are certain similarities between these two nativities, they are as fundamentally different as a royal chamber and a back alley. Even if one were to grant the thesis of Radhakrishnan[1] and others that the existence of so many parallels between the life of Jesus and the life of Buddha suggests some influence of the Buddhist stories on the Christian, the effect—apart from certain apocryphal writings—is remarkably subdued. In fact, the basic images found in the Buddhist materials are reversed, and the structures largely inverted. The Buddhist account is essentially heroic and hierarchical; the Christian account is nonheroic and nonhierarchical. The one is grandly dramatic and paradisal; the other, by comparison, quite mundane and quaintly comic. The Gospel accounts are surprisingly down-to-earth, realistic, and, one is even inclined to say, proletarian.

Though both Matthew and Luke make a special effort to authenticate Jesus' messiahship by placing him in the royal line of David through his father, Joseph, no effort at all is made to "dress up" the obscurity and lowly estate of his birth. If anything, these elements are emphasized as part of the inner plot and meaning of his nativity. They are the point of the joke, so to speak, the form of the divine folly. Jesus comes from the least of the least. He is both "low caste" and "from Nazareth," as well as from among the conquered and oppressed. As Jesus later says of himself, "Foxes have holes, and birds of the air have nests; but the Son of man has nowhere to lay his head [Matt. 8:20; Luke 9:58]." And the lowly/lonely circumstances of his birth, the motif of flight into Egypt, his rejection by ecclesiastical authorities, and his eventual crucifixion suggest something of an outcast. Jesus is seen as the reenactment of the "root out of dry ground" of Isaiah 53 who has "no form or comeliness that we should look at him, and no beauty that we should desire him," who is "despised and rejected." He is, so to speak, a fool's king.

This is not to argue the superiority of one tradition over another, but to point up affinities with comic structures and themes. In the Buddhist accounts the Buddha makes his grand entrance at the top of the social hierarchy and under the most favorable and idyllic conditions. His father's kingdom—though historically a petty domain on the border of what is now Nepal—is described in the most glorious terms. The Buddha comes, as it were, barely getting his feet wet in the human condition, and—the final point of the matter—on his way *out* of the human condition.

The Buddha is born immaculately from the side of his mother and caught in a golden net, so as not to be any more "tainted" than absolutely necessary by the lowliness of birth itself, the sexual "contamination" of the uterine channel, or the "impurities" of blood and fluid and sweat. In fact, for the tantric tradition of Tibetan Buddhism, even this immaculate birth was too lowly and defiling. He was still carried in the *womb* of a *woman*, albeit the queen Maya. As a result, the Buddha was deemed incapable of teaching the highest and most esoteric doctrines to his disciples. These had to await the coming of Padmasambhava, who was "born" a child of eight from a lotus flower!

In the biblical nativities, Jesus' birth is at the furthest remove from such royal palaces and paradisal gardens. Jesus does not make a grand entrance at the top of the human condition, but at the bottom of the bottom. In this inverted manner all human hierarchies and distinctions are set aside. They are set aside not by rising above such discriminations but by descending beneath them. Jesus is thus presented in the Gospels as one immersed in and containing the total human condition. No one could stand outside this life.

While there have been similar Christian efforts to purify, minimize, or deny the full humanity of Jesus through doctrines that run the gamut from immaculate conception to divine apparition, the basic pattern and character of the accounts is quite Hebraic. There are certain inevitable signs and wonders, and there is the hint of a divine conception. But it cannot be taken literally without contradicting the accompanying attempt at tracing Jesus' lineage to David through his father, Joseph. Such efforts at underlining the special mission of Jesus are, all in all, striking in their moderation—especially given the pious inclination toward glorification, the apologetic concern to prove messianic authenticity, and the readily available mystical temptation to gnosticize Jesus. Considering that such enticements must have been very strong, the biblical mythology of incarnation manages to remain for the most part in basic accord with the structure and implication of Jewish stories as such.

This is not to suggest that the Buddhist tradition contains no comparable elements. The later Zen sect in particular introduces a startling variety of this-worldly, nonhierarchical, and blatantly comic elements into Buddhism.[2] But in order for Zen to get to the same point and achieve the same effect, it must iconoclastically debunk the glorified heights of its own nativity. Thus Master Yun-men, after coming to that moment in the recital of the traditional nativity where the newborn Buddha stands in golden radiance to announce his arrival and supremacy, remarked to his monks, "If I had seen him at the time, I would have cut him down with my staff, and given his flesh to dogs to eat, so that peace might prevail over all the world!"

True, the Buddha comes later to renounce his royal station for the life of a casteless, wandering monk. He comes even to the brink of starving himself to death in a desperate ascetic quest for light and peace. Still, the stories of the Buddha and the stories of Jesus reveal important differences, and these differences give the Christian stories a more immediate affinity with the spirit and structure of comedy. In the Indian context, renunciation is a movement not from noble birth to being low-caste or outcaste, but to a level deemed higher and nobler and more heroic than any social casting. It is a movement beyond caste. The lowliness and poverty of Jesus—however similar—is not an incipient mendicancy or world denial. Rather, it is seen by the Gospels as an identification with those of "low estate," the poor and meek and powerless. It overcomes normal human aspirations and social distinctions not by renouncing the world and by offering methods of transcending the world, but by radical incarnation *in* the world. The total effect is not that of a spiritual high-wire act, leaving everyone murmuring and marveling in the dust below.

The Nobodies Stand Up and Are Counted

Anyone who has sat tearfully and joyfully through Chaplin's comic masterpiece *City Lights* will immediately sense the profound relationship between these biblical themes and those of comedy. Charlie the tramp, the nobody, the outcast of society with "nowhere to lay his head," becomes the strange vehicle of salvation for a blind flower girl and for a rich man bent on drowning himself. The reward for his heroism in the latter case is that he is befriended by the rich man who, in his drunkenness, takes Charlie to his mansion and treats him royally. But when the same grateful benefactor sobers up the next morning, he forgets entirely who Charlie is and has the little bum thrown out on the street.

Throughout the film, Charlie moves back and forth between the top and the bottom of the social order—as his paradoxical costuming and style had always done since Chaplin first conceived the tramp figure. As one who was both dignified gentleman and dusty vagabond, Charlie contained within a single identity the whole of the human comedy. He had universal appeal because he *was* a universal figure. No one could stand outside his comedy, for everyone had been included in the parentheses of his dress hat and floppy shoes. Moving from one side to the other within those parentheses was the rhythm of his comic action.

The blind girl selling flowers on a street corner mistakenly presumes Charlie to be one of the rich patrons of her trade. With his only coin Charlie purchases the last thing he could possibly need: a bouquet of flowers. In return he receives a pan of water in the face thrown unwittingly in his direction. He follows the blind girl to her tenement flat, where he discovers that she and her grandmother are about to be evicted because they cannot pay the rent. So Charlie—still a wealthy suitor in the imagination of the girl's blindness—finds a menial job to help out. He also learns of a doctor who has developed a new cure for blindness, but the cost is much more than both could earn in a year.

Before Charlie has much occasion to reflect on the problem, he is late to work and loses his job. In his despair he is shuffling along the sidewalk when the rich man reappears on the scene, fresh from a European vacation and drunk as ever. He backslappingly embraces his "old buddy," as if he were a long-lost college chum and insists on Charlie's coming home with him again. Reluctant at first, Charlie shrugs his shoulders and is finally persuaded. After more drinks, Charlie ventures to seize the opportunity and tell him of the blind girl. The millionaire in his drunken generosity takes out a fat roll and gives Charlie a large handful of money. But before the night is over, the rich man has begun to sober, has forgotten the gift and the identity of Charlie, and accuses him of theft. Fleeing the summoned police, Charlie manages to get the money to the girl. But as soon as he is back on the street, he is apprehended and sentenced to a prison term.

The girl, meanwhile, has used the money for an operation, recovered her sight, and opened a fashionable flower shop. All the while, she has been quite unaware that her benefactor was *not* a wealthy suitor, quite unaware that he was only an insignificant little vagabond, quite unaware that he had gone to prison so that her sight might be restored. She fondly dreams of the day when her gallant young man of means will find her again.

After serving his sentence, Charlie emerges from prison, shabbier and poorer and lonelier than ever. Then one day, as he trudges forlornly along the city streets, teased and mocked even by lowly paperboys, he happens past the window of her flower shop. His eyes light up with joy when he realizes who it is, and that she can now see. Then he stops in embarrassment and dismay as he realizes that she can see *him*.

But the girl does not—could not—recognize him. She sees only a pitiful little tramp, ragged and crumpled, making strange faces and gestures at her through the windowpane. "I've made a conquest," she laughs, and tosses him a rose. He pulls up his coat collar to avoid her eyes and hastens to move on into the shadows. She calls him back, playfully, to give him a coin. Only in the final scene does she begin to sense that this disheveled tramp was her benefactor, as she hears his voice and touches his arm and face once again, as in her blindness, and in that moment of revelation whispers, "You!" Does she also reject him in the end? The last frames show the pallid face of Charlie, the rose between his teeth, smiling timidly, hesitantly, wonderingly. We do not know.

It is a truism to note that Western civilization has long been preoccupied with power and greatness and prestige. Comedy is not the genre of our self-image or self-appraisal, or even of our salvation. Our culture heroes and "beautiful people" are those who have battled or catapulted to the top of the competitive pile, and our controlling values have wheeled onward and upward with them on the golden wings of an ideology of progress and advancement. "King of the Mountain" is the name of the game. Yet this heroic obsession with greatness and number-oneness has always stood in an awkward relationship to the biblical tradition—however much Christendom has failed to sense the awkwardness, or comedy to display it.

Measured by worldly criteria of importance and success, the entire Bible is a patchwork collection of anecdotes, genealogies, and histories of a motley people who were the nobodies of the ancient world. So much is this so that the apostle Paul, using words of the same order as the Magnificat, can exclaim, "Has not God made foolish the wisdom of the world?" The accompanying words are like a summation of the basic plot of the stories from Abraham to Joseph, to the Exodus from Egypt, to the Babylonian exile, to Jesus and the early church:

Consider your call, brethren; not many of you were wise according to worldly standards, not many were powerful, not many were of noble birth; but God chose what is foolish in the world to shame the wise, God chose what is weak in the world to shame the strong, God chose what is low and despised in the world, even things that are not, to bring to nothing things that are, so that no human being might boast in the presence of God.

—1 Corinthians 1:26-29

This is, in fact, the basic theme of this "salvation comedy," for who, after all, are the people that march in the biblical parade? Certainly not—save on the periphery—those who were the center of attention in the ancient world. Not the kings and nobility of Babylon and Persia, nor the pharaohs and architects of Egypt, nor the poets and philosophers of Greece, nor the emperors and generals and engineers of Rome. It is a parade of children, shepherds, gypsies, slaves, and refugees. It is a parade of "the maimed, the blind, and the halt." It is a parade of nobodies and the prophets of nobodies. The "chosen" of God are clearly not chosen on the basis of having the most to offer, but if anything on the basis of having nothing to offer but themselves. And the "reward" for this chosenness is often that of being the clown, the scapegoat, the butt of the joke, the mock "king of the Jews," the "fool for Christ's sake."

While there are biblical heroes, they are a curious lot indeed. So much is this so that the terms nonhero and comic hero are really more appropriate. Who, after all, are the biblical "heroes"? We meet Abraham, an obscure Mesopotamian shepherd who migrated to the little territory that was to become the doormat and corridor of successive superpowers: Assyria, Babylon, Persia, Greece, and Rome. We meet Moses, rescued son of slaves, shepherd from the back side of the desert, leading a nation of slaves out from under the might of Egypt. We meet Gideon, who with only three hundred men, armed with pitchers and ram's horns and a few good shouts, routs the threatening Midianite host. We meet Saul, who is chosen king "from the least of the tribes of Israel" and from "the humblest of all the families of the tribe of Benjamin [1 Sam. 9:21]" and who responds to his election by hiding among the baggage. We meet David, a mere shepherd boy who brings down the mighty Goliath with a single pebble and who later becomes king of a petty kingdom the size of Yellowstone National Park. Even Solomon "in all his glory" was hardly arrayed like the great kings and pharaohs of the day. And that glory became his downfall and the downfall of Israel.

There is even something picaresque about biblical stories. Insofar as picaresque heroes are relative nobodies, caught between the competing forces of the surrounding powers of the day and trying to survive in a world that seems intent on overrunning and destroying them, the history of Israel may be said to be that of a *picaro* people. The book of Esther typifies this trait as well as any. The beautiful Queen Esther, wife of the Persian Emperor Ahasuerus, "who reigned from India to Ethiopia," was after all a harem girl, of Jewish descent, of the tribe of Benjamin, whose ancestors had been taken in Babylonian captivity, an orphan whom a kinsman had adopted and arranged to have placed in a position to "find favor" with the king.

The portraits in the Gospels are little different. Jesus is heralded by the strange figure of John the Baptist crying in the wilderness, dressed in camel's skin, and eating locusts and wild honey. And Jesus as "Son of David," "Prince of Peace," and "Lord of Lords" is an odd instance of royalty indeed, from a birth to a carpenter's wife in an animal shelter, to a vagabond ministry among peasants, publicans, and sinners, to a "triumphal entry" upon an ass, to a death as a mock king with thorns for a crown and a cross for a throne. What divine foolishness is this?

The structures and *personae* of biblical stories are remarkably consistent, as are the spirit and perspective derived from them. Jesus' own disciples were hardly selected from the *Who's Who* of the Roman Empire or even from the Palestinian social register. They were uneducated fishermen, carpenters, tax collectors, underground zealots—a most motley group of people, taken from the bottom of the pile and the other side of town without careful screening, the counsel of search committees, or the examination of credentials.

Nor did Jesus have benefit of works of later sophistication, like Emily Post's *Blue Book of Social Usage*, which is much clearer about the types of people those in polite society should and should not associate with, namely, "a collection of brilliantly fashionable people." In fact, the host or hostess "who gathers in all the oddly assorted frumps on the outskirts of society cannot expect to achieve a very distinguished result." Jesus labored under a different principle of selection: "When you give a feast, invite the poor, the maimed, the lame, the blind, and you will be blessed, because they cannot repay you [Luke 14:13]."

The Whole World Turned Upside Down

When Friedrich Nietzsche, in his several tirades against Christianity, points to these elements as of the essence of the biblical tradition, he is certainly correct—though not in the dark conclusions he draws from the observation.

The Christian conception of God—God as God of the sick, God as spider, God as spirit—is one of the most corrupt conceptions of God arrived at on earth; perhaps it even represents the low-water mark in the descending development of the God type. God degenerated to the *contradiction of life*, instead of being its transfiguration and eternal *Yes*.[3]

For Nietzsche, the ultimate goal of history was "the rearing of exceptional men." And the ultimate justification of the human enterprise was in this purpose: that "the object of mankind should lie in its highest individuals. . . . Mankind ought constantly to be striving to produce great men—this and nothing else is its duty." Understandably, Nietzsche was an admirer of tragedy and enamoured of genius. And he was incensed over what he imagined to be the Christian dilution of the Greco-Roman ideals of human nobility and divine aspiration. Christianity was a religion for slaves rather than for masters, with a morality of subservient virtues: meekness, humility, forgiveness.

For those who have been witnesses of the terrible ambiguities of genius and power in the post-Nietzschean holocausts of Europe and Asia and have seen the real Superheroes and Saviors of the twentieth century, such a self-flattering humanism is pathetic at best, and lacks all sense of the comic dimensions of human greatness. In glorifying the *Übermensch*, Nietzsche has missed the fundamental comedy in the structure of many biblical scenarios. This comic structure is precisely that of a radical liberation from the arrogances of human knowledge and power. And this liberation makes possible a descent to the lowest watermark; the embrace of even the sick and the weak and the "useless"; the sudden revaluation of the "meanest creature and flower."

Far from being a "contradiction of life," this is an encompassing of the whole of life. It is an inclusion of the total human spectrum, a "transfiguration" of all limiting and restricting calculations of worth and importance, an eternal Yes to all peoples and places.

It may well be that the church has also missed the point and in that failure opened itself up to the many distortions and evils to which Nietzsche and others have addressed themselves. But to suggest that biblical faith fosters a religion of sickness, weakness, mediocrity, cowardice, and slavery, or that it debases life and individual worth, is like saying that the clown is a corrupter of morals, the jester an anarchist, and the fool a destroyer of reason! The subtle ambiguities and transformations of the biblical comedy are lost. The theme is as old as comedy itself. The ironist (eiron) appears weak and foolish yet draws upon a higher wisdom and strength, while the imposter (alazon), who is proud and boastful, is revealed as foolish and vain and is finally overcome. "And all the trees of the field shall know that I the Lord bring low the high tree, and make high the low tree, dry up the green tree, and make the dry tree flourish [Ezek. 17:24]."

In the world of the Bible, like the world of comedy, everything seems turned upside down. The whole hierarchy of human values, and the ladders of human greatness and self-importance, are inverted and collapsed. All normal expectations, and the clever stratagems of the prudent, are baffled. Servants appear in the stead of their masters and mistresses. Riffraff are admitted to the royal banquet table. The nobodies stand up and are counted. Peasants are crowned king and queen for a day. A ragged band of slaves become the chosen people of God. And the meek inherit the earth. It is a world in which beggars are more at home than the wealthy, sinners than the righteous, children than their parents, and clowns and fools than priests and scribes.

This is not, however, a simple exchange of top for bottom, of reason for irrationality, of knowledge for ignorance. Rather, everything becomes topsy-turvy so that everything may be righted. Reason is mocked so that what reason misses or suppresses may be included. All human orders are challenged, for no order is complete and final. The clown takes the place of the lowest of the low, and the fool mistakes dried peas for pearls, so that the integrity and worth of every person, thing, and moment may be defended and become the object of special wonder and delight.

Biblical Commonplaceness

When Dante entitled his fourteenth-century classic *Commedia*, he meant that it was written in the vernacular ("lax and humble" rather than lofty and stately language) and that it moved from "misery to felicity" (hell to paradise). It was not even a "divine" comedy, the divine part being added by later divines. Biblical materials do, however, form a *commedia* in both Dante's senses. But perhaps the most peculiar characteristic of nearly all biblical narratives is that they are extremely "vernacular." They belong to commonness and the common people. And they share, without awkwardness or embarrassment, in the commonplaces of everyday life. As Paul Ricoeur notes of the teachings of Jesus, "the Parables are radically profane stories. There are no gods, no demons, no angels, no miracles, no time before time . . . but precisely people like us: Palestinian landlords traveling and renting their fields, stewards and workers, sowers and fishers, fathers and sons."[4]

In the Bible as a whole, in fact, the amount of lofty spiritual instruction or devotional liturgy and edifying discourse is proportionately sparse. Instead one is often deluged with tedious genealogies, military roll calls, nuts and bolts inventories of tabernacles and temples, meticulous ceremonial codes, lists of petty kings, and an array of trifling events and curious tales. Unlike the more "spiritual" and heroic and perhaps highly mythological literatures of the world, the Bible pays attention to a host of very ordinary people doing a great many very ordinary things.

So much is this so that a modern reader, accustomed to focusing only upon the most noteworthy individuals and events, is liable to be irritated at being burdened with a mass of seemingly trivial detail and a myriad of insignificant names and stories. It may seem to anyone of discriminating taste and a fine sense of what is and is not of historical value that the Bible is an extremely poorly edited conglomeration of important but mostly unimportant materials that could better have been reduced to more sensible proportions by eliminating all these inconsequential people and incidents and concentrating only on the exceptional people and crucial events. Then it could have provided a more worthy document of the life and times of the ancient world, a register of the designs and deeds of the truly great people and nations of the ancient Near East. Instead it reads like the "Around Home" section or the obituary column of a small-town newspaper. The fact that the biblical writers and editors do not do this, however, does not necessarily suggest an inability to distinguish between the significant and the trivial. Rather, a divine set of parentheses, as it were, has been placed around all human classifications and gradations. Relative to *this* God, all distinctions between great and small have a comic pathos about them.

This is the consistent double theme that runs throughout the biblical tradition. In relation to God, all human greatness is as nothing. And yet because of this nothingness before God, even the lowliest and least is of immeasurable value. What is taken away with one hand is given back with the other, fully, graciously, and to all. In the words of Samuel Miller's description of the double miracle wrought by the clown, "it is a world of such magic and mystery that everybody becomes nobody, and the nobodies somebody." [5] It is that spiritual democratization of things which Chaplin effected again and again in his films by the simple device of tipping his hat not only to ladies and gentlemen but also to infants and trees and lampposts and milk cows.

Behold, the nations are like a drop from a bucket,
    and are accounted as the dust on the scales. . . .
All the nations are as nothing before him,
    they are accounted by him as less than nothing and emptiness. . . .
Who brings princes to nought,
    and makes the rulers of the earth as nothing. . . .
He gives power to the faint,
    and to him who has no might he increases strength.

—Isaiah 40:15, 17, 23, 29

Such is the nature of a divine foolishness which destroys the wisdom of the wise and brings to nothing the understanding of the prudent; a divine weakness in which the mighty are put down from their thrones and those of low degree are exalted; a divine comedy in which the hungry are filled and the rich are sent empty away.

Some comic theorists have argued that comedy and clowning have no transforming possibilities but rather are a conservative force, reinforcing the status quo in the act of providing temporary relief from it. Yet it is this divine comedy, whether recognized under such rubrics or not, that has been the continuing source and inspiration of much of our concern for equality, freedom, and justice for all, our compassion for the disinherited, our defense of the weak and the poor. All our social pyramids, our collective wisdoms, and our discriminations according to rank and power are set by this divine foolishness within the brackets of the comic perspective. They are taken with only a limited and provisional seriousness, not with an ultimate and absolute seriousness. They stand within that infinite, transcendent context which radically qualifies everything and in which all human distinctions are finally annulled. In Isaiah's imagery, "it is he who sits above the circle of the earth, and its inhabitants are like grasshoppers." The differences among grasshoppers, presumably, are only of tentative importance in the small world of grasshoppers.

In this divine comedy a poor woman's farthing cast inconspicuously in the temple chest may be worth more than all the benefactions of the rich. Sinners, not worthy to set foot in holy places, may be justified over those who are faithful and comfortable in their righteousness. Children may be closer to the kingdom of God than the learned and pious. Illiterates and fools may see what scribes and philosophers do not. And the most God-forsaken places may be precisely where God is to be found: Emmanuel, God with us.

    . . . We have seen
    The moon in lonely alleys make
    A grail of laughter of an empty ash-can
    And through all sounds of gaiety and quest
    Have heard a kitten in the wilderness.

                    —Hart Crane, *Chaplinesque*[6]

Chapter 9

A Happy Ending of Sorts

> *i who have died am alive again today,*
> *and this is the sun's birthday; this is the birth*
> *day of life and of love and wings: and of the gay*
> *great happening illimitably earth.*
>
> —*e.e. cummings*[1]

The happy ending has commonly been seen as one of the identifying marks of comedy. By contrast, an ending containing unresolved conflicts, self-destruction, or mutual destruction, along with a kind of relentless march of events toward such an end, has been seen as one of the identifying marks of tragedy. Tragedies terminate in death and dissolution, comedies in life and reunion. In tragedies things fall apart or decay or are destroyed by one another; in comedies things are put back together, and this happy result is often signified by a marriage, a feast, and a general mood of celebration. Tragedies produce funerals and disasters; comedies produce weddings and happily-ever-afters. But is this really the case? And does this really describe the flesh and bones of comedy?

Several decades ago F.M. Cornford advanced the intriguing thesis that the origins of both Greek comedy and tragedy were to be found in the religious drama enacted during the seasonal spring rites. Theatrical tragedy arose out of the first half of the ritual: the dying of the old year, the death and dismemberment of the fertility god, the symbolic death of the king, the return to chaos, and the resultant mood of lamentation.

But comedy arose out of the second half of the ritual: the birth of a new year and a new order, the resurrection of the god, and the reenthronement of the king. Comedy in particular picked up on the culminating movements of the spring rites: the marriage of the king and queen, the union of the fertility god and goddess, triumphal and wedding processions, feasting and revelry (*komoidia*, the revel song). The *agon* (fight, conflict) was over, and the agony became the ecstasy. Life was again victorious over death, cosmos over chaos, fertility over barrenness, spring over winter.[2]

The argument is appealing in its simplicity. Structurally and thematically many tragedies and comedies do fit the two respective phases of the festival pattern. Sophocles' *Oedipus Rex* and *Antigone* and Shakespeare's *King Lear* and *Hamlet* all come to seemingly inexorable ends, moving, however nobly, down a descending staircase into regions of darkness, death, and decay. But Aristophanes' *Birds* or Shakespeare's *Twelfth Night* or Molière's *Miser* swirl upward lightly into the sunshine of good fortune, unlikely victory, and united lovers, having won through by means of sundry mysterious forces and providential happenstances. *Hamlet* achieves multiple funerals; *As You Like It* culminates in a quadruple wedding. To tragedy belongs guilt and judgment; to comedy, love and grace.

Comic Eschatology

If so, comedy is properly "the mythos of spring" (Northrop Frye).[3] It is "an art form that arises naturally wherever people are gathered to celebrate life, in spring festivals, triumphs, birthdays, weddings, or initiations" (Susanne Langer).[4] By extension, one might see a special affinity between later Christian themes of crucifixion, resurrection, ascension, and paradise and kindred themes of comic art—themselves derived from earlier Easter rites. All the movements of such a tragi-comic structure are there in early Christian symbolism: death and dismemberment of the god/king, end of the old order, descent into hell, resurrection, new kingdom, new heavens and earth, marriage of Christ and his bride (the church), nuptial/victory feast (eucharist), ascent into paradise, and promised return in full glory and power. In these terms, tragic symbolism moves into comic symbolism and is incomplete apart from the comic conclusion. Thus Wylie Sypher can argue, "Tragic action runs through only one arc of the full cycle of the drama . . . . Consequently the range of comedy is wider than the tragic range . . . . The comic cycle is the only fulfilled and redemptive action." One might then conclude that "the drama of the struggle, death and rising—Gethsemane, Calvary and Easter—actually belongs in the comic rather than the tragic domain."[5]

In further support of this, one might point to the early Christian imagery of Jesus as the bait used to trap the devil. Or one might note that the early church did not reenact the Last Supper in a funereal atmosphere, but rather as a love feast, a sacred banquet, celebrated in the spirit of victory and rejoicing. Or one might cite the ancient custom in Greek Orthodox circles of setting aside the day after Easter as a day of merriment, a day in which joking and jesting were considered appropriate within the sanctuary because of the big joke God pulled on Satan in the resurrection. Tragedy issues in sorrow and death, salvation issues in comedy.

Such associations continue to be made in recent literary studies of the New Testament. Dan O. Via, Jr., in his *The Parables*, and more recently in his *Kerygma and Comedy in the New Testament*, draws upon the same standard characterizations of tragic and comic action. A tragic plot involves "a downward movement toward catastrophe and the isolation of the protagonist," while that of comedy "moves upward toward the well-being of the protagonist and his inclusion in a desirable society."[6] On this basis, Jesus' teachings are divided into tragic parables (e.g., the unforgiving servant) and comic ones (e.g., the prodigal son). By adding the parables to the death-burial-resurrection scenario, one is led to conclude that "the full Christian story is a comedy, but a comedy in which tragedy is included and overcome, as we see in the Prodigal Son."[7]

An immediate problem in this thesis is that—as Crossan has noted—"the world of resurrection is itself divided into Hell and Heaven, which means that tragedy and comedy are simply relocated elsewhere and frozen into everlasting and unchanging actualities."[8] Via has, in effect, granted the same point by dividing Jesus' parables into tragic and comic types, since those with "tragic" conclusions remain unredeemed. Unless one takes the universalistic position of Origen or Karl Barth, there is no "overcoming" of the tragic—as in the parable of the ten virgins, five of whom were ready and admitted to the marriage feast and five of whom arrived late and were shut out. If one is to speak of biblical stories as comic, this would seem to have less to do with endings—the way the plot "turned out"—and more to do with the manner with which life, from beginning to end, is perceived and received. Both the comic vision and the religious vision are primarily matters of spirit, not form.

There are also problems from the side of comedy. While many tragedies and comedies may be fitted into the contrasting structures of downward and upward movement, not all may be. And even those that seem to fit do so with important qualifications. As scholars from Hegel to Walter Kerr have pointed out, the original concept of tragic action was the *whole* of the ritual movement, not just its first half.[9] Both tragedy and comedy as we know them developed in the Dionysian festival—and therefore are dedicated to spring and fertility—with tragedy preceding comedy by half a century. In early tragedy the final goal was to achieve reconciliation and renewal after having worked through certain points of conflict (*agon*). The function of the first two plays in the tragic trilogy was to identify certain "worlds in collision," to express the appropriate lamentations, then to bring the opposing forces or virtues into a saving resolution in the final play. Thus in the third play of Aeschylus' *Oresteia*, justice is achieved, compensation is made, and forces are reconciled. Or, in the Promethean trilogy, though only the first play is extant, we presume that somehow both Prometheus and Zeus are accommodated. And even though in a number of Greek tragedies no natural means of arriving at a resolution presented itself, the playwright was not above the use of a deus ex machina to resolve his dilemmas abruptly. This conclusion, in turn, was followed by a humorous satyr play, with goat-men or horse-men parodying some heroic legend—as in Euripides' *Cyclops* which *satirizes* an episode from Homer's *Odyssey*. In this manner the tragic performance had not only a happy ending but also a comic ending of sorts.

The principal reason we have tended to view tragedy otherwise is that the prevailing dramatic form from Sophocles through Shakespeare to the present has been the depiction of conflicts in their unredeemed agony. A certain course of action is tenaciously carried through to the bitter end. A certain heroism is displayed, but it is purchased at great expense. A certain justice is achieved, but it is harsh, and its lessons are painful and hard won. If Aeschylus had produced only *Prometheus Bound*, we would have had a similar result: a dramatic action locked in a "tragic" antithesis or ambiguity, with no synthesis offered or seemingly offerable, relentlessly moving toward heroic self-sacrifice in a fateful collision of forces.

Comedy, however, is no more tied to the happy ending than tragedy is to an unhappy one. If, in fact, comedy manages a happy ending, it is in some measure in jest. As in the many ingeniously contrived conclusions of Molière's plays, where suddenly and miraculously everything works out beyond anyone's wildest imaginations, the final harmony of forces and integration of loose ends is just too good to be true. And that is half the point, and the basis for laughter, in comedy. We may be permitted to indulge our fantasies, to symbolize our dreams and desires, and to ritualize the most ambitious finale. But all this is accompanied, as if there were persistent crickets in the woodwork, by a retinue of built-in comic signals that retain or restore a sense of reality. Walter Kerr's description of a Molière ending does him—and comedy in general—perfect justice: "so many long-lost children restored to their parents, so many friends who have not met in twenty years meeting now, so many people who have been meeting daily without recognizing one another suddenly blinking twice and gasping 'You!', so many secret documents so opportunely revealed."[10] The ending is so complete that we laugh out of sheer delight and sheer incredulity over such an impossible network of happy coincidences so cleverly made possible on the ritual stage.

When the down-and-out Chaplin in *Easy Street* is converted in a Bowery mission (that is, he falls in love with the organist), he vows to go straight and make something of himself. He becomes a police officer. His first assignment, without any training and without even knowing the front of his police hat from the back, is to the worst beat in the city, Easy Street. Despite the odds, he succeeds in defeating the local Goliath through a series of tricks and bluffs. By the end of the film the underdog has gained such an upper hand that the absolute chaos of Easy Street is turned into absolute order, and everything is love and peace and flowers.

In viewing such pleasant preposterousness relative to city toughs and street gangs and thieves and related varieties of urban ills, one laughs—joyfully, to be sure—over the symbolic triumph of David over Goliath and the Philistines. The spirit is uplifted at this sudden realization of the kingdom of God on earth, the New Jerusalem in the New York Bowery. But one also laughs just as heartily because that isn't the *way* things happen and that isn't *what* happens. In fact, at the end of the film, when the local thugs and scoundrels, including Goliath himself, are all dressed up in Sunday suits, politely escorting their wives and girl friends to the new mission established on Easy Street itself, one laughs over the spotlessness of the finale in a newfound nostalgia. Remarkably enough, it is not the "nostalgia for paradise" — which has just been vented — but the nostalgia for a little realistic chaos here and there! The ending is so clean and orderly that we laugh in an amused sense of its absurdity and in a realization that it is so finished that the action and drama is now over forever. We begin wishing to see just one more brawl in the middle of Easy Street, one more difficulty to test us. Secretly we pray, May the Lord of Disorder revisit us!

While comedy may end as paradisally as a romance or a fairy tale, with hero and heroine married and living happily ever after, if it does so it is with a knowing wink and a mischievous grin. We know that that is not the way life is, has been, or is ever likely to be. But we are permitted the beatific vision and the momentary enjoyment of such utopian circumstances, while at the same time being alerted by the comic muse not to get too lost in sentimental idylls. This alerting, however, comes not out of sarcasm or cynicism but out of a humor that lies between fideism and despair. And it does not come as a cold slap in the face. It is administered through that very different sort of jolt — the joke, the comic twist, the humorous aside, or simply the preposterous finish.

When Aristophanes in *The Birds* has Hopeful — who has at first set out with his friend Plausible to live a simple life among the birds — soaring by play's end to the top of the highest heaven as king of the universe, we know that our feathers are being pulled. The comic climax is hope*lessly* *implausible*. Or when Molière masterminds one of his elaborately contrived endings, where all the pieces suddenly move into place and perfect love and justice prevail, we shake our heads in disbelief. We know that it is a clever trick, an ingenious farce, and we laugh. Our wildest dreams have been simultaneously indulged and debunked.

In *The Navigator*, Buster Keaton and his love are surrounded by cannibals. They are about to escape in an outrigger but instead fall in the water. With their arms around each other, they begin to disappear beneath the surface, destined to drown in a lover's embrace. Then suddenly they begin to ascend. At that precise moment a submarine happens to be surfacing, and they reappear for their watery grave, standing on what turns out to be the ship's hatch. Deus ex machina.

In a sense, it does not matter whether the comic victory is ever achieved in the real world, whether good finally conquers evil, or justice everlastingly prevails over ruthless power, or the meek at last and invincibly inherit the earth. Such is the peculiar mythological requirement of linear views of history which can only justify time and history, flesh and blood, as that which leads to perpetual progress or some final bliss. In the fantasy of comedy, the human dream has already been achieved, and is achieved, in every comic ritual—*symbolically*. But it is not achieved in such a way as to freeze life and its ongoing dreams. It permits the game to be played again and again. Its mission is not to annul history or conquer death or obviate suffering but to renew and celebrate life. While in the real world, hope is often defeated and evil often triumphant, in the world of the spirit, hope eternal is nevertheless preserved. In the comic rite all the emotions and satisfactions of a real victory are there, to be repeated like the Easter liturgy itself, in all subsequent symbolic victories. And this is the redemptive catharsis of comedy. As Cedric Whitman has argued with respect to Aristophanic comedy,

the world as it is perhaps cannot be transcended; but the comic hero is not stopped by that. He invents his own world and then subdues it . . . This is, indeed, madness, but it is poetic madness; and it is neither directly moral or immoral. It is an heroic absurdity, the absurdity of the helpless little self out-absurding the incorrigible world.[11]

The same self-consciousness that presents the problem of suffering and evil to human reflection—animals do not worry over it—is the self-consciousness that is capable of transcending the problem in comic myth and ritual itself. In the world of the spirit, the dragons may always be slain and the villains properly vilified. Only among those who insist, as a prerequisite of celebration, upon literal historical victories now or forthcoming does prosaic fact triumph over poetic license and comic absurdity. And we are left with either a stubborn clinging to utopian dreams or a disenchanted cynicism and despair.

The Not-so-happy Ending

But comedies by no means always have a happy ending. The comic ending may be at the furthest remove from a fantastically or even moderately successful conclusion. Perhaps nothing works out, the project is a failure, everything goes wrong, and the final scene is anything but blissful. Now where are we? Buster Keaton in *Cops* goes to great lengths to make something of himself in order to win the affections of the mayor's daughter. But when, after heroic efforts to become a success and after being successful at least in eluding the police through much of the film, she still spurns him, he throws himself to the mob of angry police officers. The last image: a tombstone with Keaton's hat atop.

Laurel and Hardy begin the film *Big Business* with the finest of intentions as Christmas-tree salespeople. Christmas cheer and the spirit of free enterprise are in the air. But through a series of misunderstandings with a homeowner who is totally uninterested in purchasing a tree, the film moves through a wild escalation of hostilities. Laurel and Hardy begin destroying his house piece by piece, as the homeowner destroys their truck and load of evergreens piece by piece. By the end of the film the house and yard is a shambles, the truck is a pile of scrap, and the homeowner, after running madly around beating the jumbled remains of the truck with a stick, writhes orgiastically on the ground in the pile of mangled Christmas trees. Happy holidays!

One would be hard pressed to discover the supposed hallmarks of comedy in this bit of bedlam and rubble: happy ending, reunion, marriage, celebration. There is a reconciliation of sorts effected at the end by a police officer who has incredulously observed the donnybrook. The parties shed tears of remorse and shake hands. Hardy then offers the former homeowner a cigar as a gesture of friendship. It turns out to be a trick cigar that explodes in his face! Even in the midst of total failure and destruction, one last joke cannot be resisted.

In between the riches and rags endings for comedies are those comedies that settle for smaller successes or eventuate in more limited failures. The hero doesn't get the girl, but he does get the horse. And perhaps, he decides philosophically, the horse will prove to be a more reliable and less costly companion anyway. So he kisses the horse and rides off. Or he gets the girl, but not the one he had his heart set on. Though she is not the ravishing creature that had set him swooning in the first place, that difference may not be so noticeable with the lights out. He accepts the realities of his fate with a toss of the head and a *c'est la vie.* He may blurt out a quip or two to express his disappointment, but also in a refusal to be destroyed by it.

In Keaton's frontier classic *Go West*, the plot is much like that of most Westerns, before and since. The hero (Keaton, after a fashion) vanquishes the bad guys (also after a fashion) and rescues the damsel in distress, who happens to be the daughter of a wealthy old rancher. A just and equitable finale naturally suggests itself in the form of the hero receiving the girl and some financial blessing as a reward. And circumstances seem to be leading in that very direction. The old rancher congratulates Keaton, and the daughter winsomely flutters her eyelashes. But Keaton doesn't know quite what to do with girls. The final scene is unsurpassed. Keaton is being driven off in the rancher's touring car. In the front seat are the father and his daughter. In the back seat, Keaton and a cow!

In another of Keaton's comedies he is putting the finishing touches on a little wooden bungalow. He stands back to survey his handiwork, and decides to give a nail one final hammerblow for good measure. It brings the whole structure collapsing around him. But the stone-faced Keaton is nonplussed. When the front wall of the house fell toward him he was standing in the spot framed by the open doorway, and he emerges unscathed. One must be thankful for life's little blessings.

There are also those comedies that end ambiguously, like *City Lights*, where we shall never know if Charlie and the girl he had rescued from blindness ever got together. We are left with that unforgettably ambivalent face: Charlie, with a hesitant-hopeful-fearful smile, rose between his teeth, wistfully happy, yet shy, embarrassed, wondering—as we are left wondering. A whole gamut of opposite possibilities and emotions are captured in that one final enigmatic moment. And that is precisely what is enjoyable about the ending: its unresolved and unspoiled ambiguity.

To this we must add all those comedies that show us at first a completely successful ending. The perfect caper has been consummated. As in *The Lavender Hill Mob*, the unrobbable bank has been robbed after years of meticulous research and brilliant scheming carried out with clockwork precision. But the latch on the suitcase in the rumble seat of the getaway car was carelessly closed, and the wind scatters a trail of bills behind the speeding vehicle. One tiny bit of fallibility brings the whole escapade to nought. Or, a romance is properly culminated in an idyllic wedding, and the swooning lovers are off to Niagara Falls and honeymoon bliss. But one final scene cannot be resisted. It is captioned "And They Lived Happily Ever After." The wife is in curls and disheveled bathrobe; the baby is screaming; the mother-in-law is busily berating; and the husband is slouched, T-shirted, unshaven and grumpy. The last shot shows the husband back at the scene of the honeymoon, standing on an observation deck beside the falls, contemplating suicide. Finis.

Why such treatments of the ending, whether sublime, disastrous, or any of several shadings in between? Because comedy impulsively returns to the real world, real people, real situations, real possibilities, real pasts, presents, and futures. And yet it is not just any real world. Comedy returns to the real world with a special flourish of its own. The real world, after all, can be harsh, cruel, malicious, boring, depressing, hateful, violent, destructive. So it is the real world, seen in a special way, infused with a special spirit, offering a special grace. It is not paradise. But it is also not the ordinary world as ordinarily perceived. It is a world in which all the winnings and losings, dreams and dreadings, are appropriated comically. It is a world in which comedy has the last word and the last laugh. Implicit in its vision is the intimation of a world that—though not quite one or another of the usually contradictory paradises we have imagined—could be better if that vision were more pervasive. And, as James Sully has suggested, "while satire, sarcasm and their kind seem to be trying to push things away, or at least to alter them, humour, curiously enough, looks as if it were tenderly holding to the very world which entertains it."[12]

There is a further reason for the multiplicity of comic endings. Comedy does not *need* any particular ending at all. The comic hero may be victor or victim, trickster or tricked, or just a vagabond wandering in and out of fortune and misfortune. Stan Laurel could end an escapade in a daffy grin or a woeful sob or a squeal of mischievous delight. His pal Oliver easily slid back and forth between proudly and pompously wiping his hands over a momentary triumph, theatrical outrage over the latest bit of bungling, and quivering like a frightened child caught with his hands in the cookie jar. Where it all ended was arbitrary, as all storied endings are arbitrary, as life itself is arbitrary. But whatever the ending, one could be assured that comedy was going to play with it, turn it over and around and even upside down.

Freud argued that humor is the capacity for transferring energy from unpleasurable circumstances and feelings to pleasurable ones. And that is certainly part of the secret. As in the tale of the Lithuanian Yiddish fool, Khabad, whose house caught fire, when the house was going up in flames, instead of running about in a panic as his neighbors were doing, he began to laugh. "At last," he exclaimed, "I have my revenge on the cockroaches!"[13] But the reverse of Freud's thesis is also true: Comedy takes pleasurable circumstances and reminds us of unpleasurable ones. Comedy insists on a "reality principle." In this case, if it happened to be some villain's house burning, the cockroaches might well be shown transferring themselves to the house of an overly gleeful underdog.

The comic spirit seems capable of standing apart from and adjusting to whatever the circumstances, with a shrug or a wink inserted somewhere or other. It takes on both famine and plenty, funerals and weddings, triumphs and defeats. This, in fact, is an expression of one of the most saving attributes of human nature: the capacity of freedom and transcendence that enables us to laugh and joke and see the humor in things great and small. It is a resilience of spirit which can reassert itself when life is coming up daffodils or coming up dandelions or coming up with nothing at all. Even Emmett Kelly's "forlorn and melancholy little hobo who always got the short end of the stick and never had any good luck at all . . . never lost hope and just kept on trying."[14] The comic is like the child's toy that is weighted at the bottom and often painted with the face of a clown or some humorous character, which however struck down or laid to rest bobs straight up again.

The "sense of regain," as Harold Watts called it, is central to comedy —though not in the niggardly way he used it: "A sense of regaining what the more cowardly part of our natures had feared might be gone forever . . . a universe compact of familiar objects and painless ideas." Nor is it an unheroic "retreat from the precipices where one stands to talk to the gods," offering us instead a place "to be cradled, to forego mental and spiritual growth in favor of a lively jounce." Nor is it merely the regain of "a commonplace set of values," a "mediocre kind of sanity," and the comfort of "current platitudes."[15] What is regained is a sense of perspective and balance relative to the self, its circumstances, and its world. Whether the focus of the moment is on the sublime or the commonplace, the exceptional or the mediocre, the profound or the platitudinous, comedy bobs straight up again.

Tragic visions may point grandly at human courage and freedom and dig in for heroic confrontations and last stands with "head bloody, but unbowed." But it is in comedy that we prove to be fully free to laugh at and take on the world. And this requires no small courage and size of soul. If the book of Job may be said to approach the comic domain, it is not in the final verses in which Job receives back everything that has been taken from him, but rather at the point when everything is lost and he nevertheless affirms, "The Lord gave, the Lord has taken away; blessed be the name of the Lord [Job 1:21]."

The Comic Transformation

There is a scene at the end of one of Chaplin's early shorts, *The Tramp*, which in a single moment captures the heart of comic courage and freedom. It was Chaplin's first full-fledged use of the tramp figure and exploitation of its ambiguous possibilities. The film begins with the tramp walking down a dusty road, being twice knocked to the ground by a passing car and twice getting up to dust himself off with the whisk broom he seems to carry for such purposes. He then chances on a farmer's daughter on her way into town for shopping being set upon by three thieves. But although he rescues the maiden and her money, and although she escorts the hero back to her home and introduces him to her father, he does not get the girl or her father's financial blessing. For a reward he is offered work. An affair of the heart seems for a time to be in the making, but the tramp is soon disappointed, for what he thought was love proves to be only pity and girlish playfulness. When her dapper boyfriend drives up from the city and bursts on the scene, backslapping the father and embracing the daughter, the little tramp is quickly forgotten. Instead of the little beast being released from his lowly estate and transformed by a maiden's kiss into a handsome, dashing prince, a different transformation occurs. It is a comic transformation.

The final frames of the film show the tramp at first sadly scribbling her a note and dejectedly leaving the farmhouse. He says an awkward good-bye to the girl, who is busily chatting with her boyfriend. The boy has gotten the girl, but it is the wrong boy. The tramp is offered money by the jovial boyfriend, but he refuses it. Forlornly he trudges back down the dusty road on which he came into the picture. Then suddenly it happens. In the final seconds of the film the tramp straightens up, kicks up his heels, and walks briskly, even jauntily, away. *That* is the courage and the transformation. The tramp discovers, and the viewer discovers, that the truly human figure was there all along, truly free in spirit, risen above the ups and downs of life. In a sense there was no need for miraculous transformation into a prince, no need to be snuggled into this or that human order, no need for the fine garments and castles (or farmhouses) and happily-ever-afters. The tramp was fully human and fully free, just as he was. Here was a humanity, an uncorrupted and uncompromised genuineness, that no amount of cultivated city-slickness could match and no amount of marital bliss could purchase. Dirt and all, and all in all, *this* was the prince.

If comedy may be said to have an eschatology at all, it is a very "realized" eschatology. "Paradise" is to be experienced *now*, in the midst of the turbulence of life. In Chaplin's last tramp film, *Modern Times*, produced in the depression years, the homeless tramp and a homeless orphan girl (Paulette Goddard) find a place to live. Both are ecstatic over it. We are then shown the object of their enthusiasm: a flimsy, abandoned shack along the waterfront. As Charlie enters, a ceiling beam falls on his head. The mirage of a table collapses when he leans on it. The chair he sits on drops through the floorboards. When he nonchalantly relaxes against the wall, he falls through into the water outside. "It's a paradise!" she exclaims. And so it is, a comic paradise.

Yes, there are comedies with perfect endings, even all-too-perfect endings. The difference is that they are, after all, *comedies*. We know, or should know, that what has been given with one hand is to be taken away with the other. Or, better, it is both given and taken away in the same dramatic motion. Paradisaical episodes and happily-ever-afters are presented humorously and as fantasies, and therefore in such a way as not to lose sight of or devalue the actualities of everyday life. Comic eschatology returns life to the present moment and its circumstances, be they ever so humble. The game is not suspended, even in triumph. The *game* is celebrated, not just an occasional victory. The game is always allowed to begin again, in some new form perhaps or in the same old form. "Comic eschatology," as Crossan has argued, "restores the world *sub specie ludi*." Comedy is "the epiphany of play."[16]

In all this comic play, a fundamental yes is said to the world, despite its problems and tensions and incongruities. The result is not a low view of life as irredeemably absurd—though comedy does employ its share of absurdities. One is not tormented by the failure of life to live up to all the plots and plans and purposes laid out for it. Comedy does not proceed from or lead to a sense of futility, alienation, or despair over the mysterious meanderings of our lives. It is true that certain playwrights—Chekhov, Beckett, Ionesco, Pirandello, Pinter, Albee, and kindred spirits have used the comic to show that life is absurd. Their "comedies" are thus bittersweet at best, a "comic grimace," as Pirandello called them, leaving one not knowing quite whether to laugh or cry. There are humorous lines and comic situations, yet the overall effect is not comic. The result is not a celebration of life or a call for justice or a renewal of faith and hope, but a void in the pit of the stomach, a void that reaches out throughout the universe.

Satire, to be sure, uses the comic to prove that certain actions or beliefs are absurd. And irony uses the comic to clarify the absurdity in our incongruities and self-contradictions. But comedy as such uses the absurd to prove that life is comical. And it finds some basis, one way or another and somewhere or other, for enjoying the humor in it. Absurdity is not the meaning of comedy but the method. If matters were otherwise, then, as G. K. Chesterton insisted, "in a world where everything is ridiculous, nothing can be ridiculed. . . . If life is really so formless that you cannot make head nor tail of it, you cannot pull its tail; and you certainly cannot make it stand on its head."[17] Comedy presupposes some frame of reference, some article of faith, some vision of hope, some sense of mystery that has not been reduced to an absurdist credo.

The world of comedy is not the world of Robbet-Grillet's *Jealousy,* where nothing significant happens because there is no longer any standard of significance, or of Sartre's *Nausea,* where in the absence of a meaning for life Roquentin is left with contemplation of suicide in disgust over the dirty hodgepodge of chaotic phenomena around him. It is not the world of Beckett's plotless "sequence" of rambling incidents, where, as in *Waiting for Godot,* it hurts Vladimir to laugh, or Henry in *Embers* can only muster a "long horrible laugh," or Arsene in *Watt* offers but the dregs of the cup of laughter, "the bitter, the hollow, and the mirthless." Nor is it the world of Ionesco, "in which all human behavior tells of absurdity and all history of absolute futility . . . so what possible reaction is there left, when everything has ceased to matter, but to laugh at it all?"[18] This mirthless laughter, which Beckett crowns as "the *risus purus,*" the "laugh of laughs," is not comedy but the death rattle of comedy.

The laughter of comedy is not the hollow laughter of cynicism or the anguished laughter of despair, masking bitter disappointment underneath and making obscene gestures to the sky. The effect is not that of some fond dream shattered, some belief disillusioned, some abyss opened up. Even in those comedies that end ambiguously or in defeat, one is left with a distinct sense of faith renewed and hope rekindled. A stubborn affirmation of life wells up irresistibly in the comic vision, a heroic "courage to be" (Tillich) that refuses to be daunted or destroyed. Comedy, as Christopher Fry has insisted, is an escape, to be sure, yet "not from truth but from despair; a narrow escape into faith. It says, in effect, that, groaning as we may be, we move in the figure of a dance, and, so moving, we trace the outline of the mystery."[19]

Chapter 10

The Game and the Adventure

*The reason he did these things was that
mortals might always laugh,
whenever his story is told,
as long as there is an earth.*
—Menomini storyteller

The arbitrariness in the fortunes and misfortunes of life is a universal human experience. No matter how egalitarian or advanced a society, there are still the advantaged and disadvantaged, intelligent and retarded, attractive and unattractive, nimble and lame, long-lived and short-lived, and every other gradation to which flesh and spirit are heir. Individual life as well, no matter how privileged on any scale of value, is a mixed array of ups and downs, successes and failures, happy and unhappy coincidences.

In the comic tradition, these elements of randomness and happenstance that swirl through much of our lives are made the special focus of attention. They are elements that our theologies often ignore—or attribute to sinister forces—in favor of a singular emphasis upon cosmic orders, divine plans, historical patterns, and ultimate destinies. Yet despite our most concerted efforts at shaping things into a rational, orderly, meaningful whole, life is not notably intelligible or predictable or just. The "principles" of uncertainty and indeterminacy (Heisenberg) are also hard at play. Hence all those quirks of fate, meandering plots, curious surprises, playful fantasies, petty interruptions, and odd circumstances that proliferate themselves in comedies. Comedy comes directly to terms with the arbitrariness of life, without any quick sweep under the rug or elaborate attempt at rationalization—in fact, by accepting this as essential to the adventure itself. Apart from this side of things, there would be no adventure, no risk, no challenge, no drama. Absolute equality and predictability would guarantee absolute monotony. If in the beginning God created order out of chaos (Genesis 1:2), God also created chaos. Chaos is the other side of order.

In the world of games, we readily acknowledge that the essence of a game is the interplay between structure and arbitrariness. To the degree that the elements of unpredictability and potential defeat are diminished, the enjoyment of the sport is diminished and it becomes no contest at all. A game without these qualities would become totally pointless, meaningless, and boring. Although games develop considerable orderliness and equality through rules and regulations, if there is no possibility for a bad bounce or a lucky break, no chance for underdogs and long shots, no room for worry or hope, we say that this would take all the fun out of it, that it would not be worth playing, and even that it would be unfair.

The ancient symbol of this perception of life is the trickster—ancestor to all clowns and fools and comic heroes. The trickster has been known in many cultures under many names and forms, both animal and human. In a majority of tales the trickster is identified with an animal suggesting clever and wily traits: coyote, wolf, fox, raven, raccoon, badger, spider, jay. He is almost always "he"—perhaps in part because the trickster is a vagabond, and vagabondage has been much more of a male occupation and possibility than a female one. The trickster is an individualist and a wanderer, a "lone wolf" who survives by his own cunning and prowess. He is a master of camouflage and disguise. Sometimes he is literally a shapeshifter, with the capacity to turn himself into a variety of forms—like Hermes who escaped detection by slipping through the keyhole as a mist.

But for all the trickster's bagful of tricks, he is also noted for his ignorance and foolishness. Sometimes he outwits others, sometimes he is outwitted, sometimes he outwits himself, and sometimes an unforeseen turn of events outwits everybody. Yet clever or foolish, the trickster manages to survive to pick up either the spoil or the pieces.

In the trickster we may be seeing, as some scholars have speculated, one of the oldest figures in all mythology. [1] If so, he is one of the earliest images of human existence. Yet he is not just a relic from the remote past. We find him in the Greek Prometheus who tricks the Olympian gods and steals the sacred fire of civilization for mortals, and in the biblical serpent, who tempts Eve to eat the forbidden fruit with the promise of godlikeness. He is quite familiar in the Negro tales of Bre'r Rabbit or the boyish forms of Tom Sawyer and Huckleberry Finn. We have known him in Chaplin's tramp, in the hobo, and in the flimflam man. Trickster themes are also common throughout the history of clowning and comedy in the use of pranks, practical jokes, sleight of hand, or some trick of fate as stock comic devices. The world of the trickster is, in fact, most alive and well in the legion of modern film cartoons, some of which consist almost entirely of tricks and "shapeshifting," from the intrepid Bugs Bunny, who always gets the best of every situation, to the give-and-take of endless cat-and-mouse episodes, to the hapless coyote in *Roadrunner*, whose every trick results in personal disaster.

Wandering Within the Great Food Chain of Being

In the tales of the trickster, the trick is the basic metaphor through which life is perceived. The choice of metaphor is a primitive, yet remarkably profound one. Tricking and being tricked are inevitable features of the struggle of creatures to survive. This is the nature of life as we know it and experience it. The world is "full of tricks," life "plays tricks on us," and the business of living is itself a "tricky business." The phrases and images are as modern as they are ancient.

The image of the trickster and the metaphor of the trick may no longer be a self-conscious part of our symbolic repertoire. And in their original form they no doubt belonged to the earliest cultural strata of food-gathering, hunting, and fishing, where the caprices of nature's food supply, and human techniques of stalking, baiting, and trapping, easily suggested trickery as a fundamental element of life. Yet they still open up dimensions that more characteristic twentieth-century images and metaphors, with their heavily rational bias (including the irrational and absurd), do not.

The majority of trickster myths present a hero of sorts, a "character" to be more accurate, who wanders from one adventure and misadventure to another. This itinerant hero has neither a clear place in the "scheme of things" nor a clearly defined social identity. In his nomadic meanderings he is involved in a miscellaneous series of episodes that have little logical or dramatic connection, except that they are usually concerned with survival and with getting in and out of tight spots. The trickster seems always to be hungry and in the process of trying to obtain food, eating it in large quantities as if it were his last meal, or having it stolen or conned away by other creatures.

One can easily see in the trickster the archaic ancestor to the Chaplin of *Behind the Screen* (1915) on a lunch break with fellow stagehands—but without a lunch. One stagehand has spread out great stacks of sandwiches before him, another has unwrapped the remains of a leg of beef, while another has brought a large bunch of onions. In the midst of this cornucopia, poor Charlie sits wistfully with but two empty slices of bread, trying to determine the best way to snitch a bite of beef from the end of the bone or to steal a sandwich from the pile, while avoiding the onions. The symbolic—and existential—distance between an ancient trickster and a twentieth-century-film tramp is not very great after all, nor for that matter is he very far removed from any of us. The trickster is life reduced to its rudiments: the arbitrary fortunes of life, the uncertainties of life, the struggle of life, life feeding upon life, life in defense of life, the fundamental nakedness of our life.

For all his prowess, not without cause is the trickster called, and does he call himself, "the foolish one." In a number of tales told about him, he is bungling, hoodwinked, teased, distracted, or taken advantage of. In many Indian tribes of the Southwest, the coyote was represented at ritual dances as a clownish figure, clever, to be sure, but whose antics, mistakes, confusions, and howling set the spectators "howling" with delight. Among the Algonquins, the trickster falls into a hollow tree and only manages to escape by throwing himself out, piece by piece, from a small hole in the side of the tree. In the Winnebago tales, the trickster gets his arm caught in a tree fork while trying to stop the tree from squeaking in the wind, and as a result some passing wolves help themselves to a free meal of raccoon, which the trickster has just trapped and prepared. Later he gets his head stuck in an elk's skull and has to trick people into thinking he is a spirit that will do wonderful things for them if they will break open the skull and let him out.

The trickster is much like an overgrown child, orphaned and wandering in the wilderness, trying to learn how to cope with his environment, fending for himself in a world of competing forces and creatures, with no foreknowledge of how best to proceed. As the fox says to the trickster in the Winnebago cycle, "the world is going to be a difficult place to live in." The trickster does not doubt it for a minute. He has, as it were, been thrown into existence—as are we all. He awakes to find himself existing and sees no obvious niche for himself or any obvious plan of action, but he is nevertheless determined to make the best of it. He lays claim to no special revelations, neither does he complain that he has not been provided with any. In the absence of a ready-made blueprint for his existence, he learns through trial and much error. Yet he shows no particular resentment over these circumstances, or any inclination to speculate on how things might or should have been. He conveys no sense of being condemned to ignorance, to earth, to the flesh, to thorns and thistles, or to freedom. Life is taken as it comes, and with gusto he throws himself into existence.

Even when the trickster acts stupidly or is outsmarted, he is not entirely defeated and dispirited but possesses a childlike resiliency that enables him to get back up and be back at it again, without grudge or malice, a little bruised or hungry perhaps, but also a little wilier and wiser. Rather than being weighed down by his misfortunes or limitations or by the apparent inequities and injustices of life, he takes life as a challenge and makes a game of it. All the while, the setting of his adventures, winning or losing, is a decidedly comic one. It leads to laughter as well as to tears and dismay.

There is in these materials a very candid yet good-humored acknowledgment of the actual conditions of human life. Though one might point to a certain givenness to existence and its possibilities, the knowledge and power necessary for survival have to be wrested from nature, and in some degree from one another. And this the trickster sets out to do, groping and grasping his way along. For him the most basic elements of food and shelter are not freely given, as by an indulgent parent, or in some garden paradise where all things needful grow in spontaneous abundance. He must forcibly pluck the fruit and contend with a variety of competing forces in so doing. Pipe dreams aside, the necessities of life must in some degree be taken and defended by trickery of sorts.

In a Chinook tale, Coyote conspires with Skunk to feign illness, and when various animals come to sing cures over him, he gasses them! Life preying upon life—as life has been doing for a billion years or so—is a series of tricks. The hunter uses a disguise in order to trick the hunted. The hunted disguises itself in order to trick the hunter. And in the great food "chain of being" the hunter in turn may well become the hunted.

As Mark Twain put it in *Roughing It*, "All things have their uses and their part and proper place in Nature's economy: the ducks eat the flies; the flies eat the worms; the Indians eat all three. The wildcats eat the Indians; the white folks eat the wildcats; and thus all things are lovely."[2] *This* is the world God has created, though few have been willing to rejoice and be glad in it.

> And God said: Let there be sprats to gobble the gnats
> So that the sprats may nourish the rats
> Making them fat, fine food for the cats.
> —Leonard Bernstein, *Mass*

Theodicy

When more systematic mythologies came to insist on impeccable creators who created more agreeable and intelligible worlds, or developed idealized culture heroes from whom weaknesses and fumblings had been culled away, the appeal of the trickster was diminished. He tended either to be refashioned in these terms or turned into a more devilish individual. If the former—as among the Pomo and Yuki tribes of California—he became a much more straight and stereotyped figure (high god, divine assistant, or great hero), gaining in reverence and predictability but losing in color and complexity. If the latter—as among the Maidu of California—he became the spoiler who had played a variety of "mean tricks" on the world, and thus introduced evil and disorder.

Sometimes the trickster was split into two opposing figures, a good, benevolent creator and a malevolent or foolish one—as among the Iroquois and the Klamath. And sometimes his stories were simply pushed aside as secular tales, tolerated by priests and shamans "for entertainment only," but not to be taken seriously, and certainly not credited with mythological validity (Southwestern Plains tribes).

Yet in any of these developments, however elevated or elevating their motives, some important perceptions came to be lost. The earlier trickster had not been the symbolic product of efforts to overcome the basic conditions of life, or to lament them, or to rail against them, or to despair over them, or even to rationalize them—that is, try to make sense out of them and render them reasonable and just. While scholars such as Mircea Eliade have attempted to argue for the universality of the "nostalgia for paradise" and of the belief in a "fallen" humanity and cosmos,[3] the primary mythology of the trickster did not participate in this vision. The trickster did not imagine or offer perfect, model worlds, as if being thankful for some world *other* than the immediate one—in the past, the heavens, or the future—were somehow the appropriate manner of registering gratitude for life and the joy of life. He was a figure through whom life was accepted in all its resistance to being as predictable and equitable and orderly as we might have preferred. He came, like Kazantzakis' Zorba the Greek, with a

savage bubbling laugh from a deep, deep well-spring deeper than the bowels of man, a laugh which at critical moments spurted and was able to demolish (did demolish) all the barriers—morality, religion, home-land—which that wretched poltroon, man, had erected around him in order to hobble with full security through his miserable smidgen of life."[4]

Noble efforts at theodicy and theologizing history have been made, relative to individual fortunes, the fate of nations, and the vagaries of history. Various formulations have been offered in an effort to lend a semblance of justice or rationality to the inequities of life: sin and judgment, providence and predestination, karma and reincarnation, the fates and the stars. But the arbitrariness of life, which in the biblical context is expressed in the theme of "the will of God," is not easily reduced by offering apologetic rationales. "I have chosen whom I have chosen" admits of no higher court of appeal in Reason and its reasons.

Our respective "lots" in life do resemble the casting of lots, except in the most general sense that all suffer and die or that God "makes his sun rise on the evil and on the good, and sends rain on the just and on the unjust [Matt. 5:45]." There is always, therefore, in any organization of experience—however well organized—a point at which reasons are finally exhausted, answers raise as many questions as they solve, and arguments begin to appeal to "paradox," "the limitations of reason," "inscrutability," "mystery," "miracle," or "having faith."

It is some point such as this from which, more directly and with less torture of mind, the tales of the trickster proceed, without any offer of some well-hidden cosmic plan or elaborate attempts to justify the ways of God to the ways of humankind, but with a comic sense of playing in the rough and tumble of life.

The trickster may seem an archaic figure from a savage past that higher civilizations and religions have moved beyond. Yet human progress has not made the trickster obsolete. If anything, our scientific and technological successes have shifted the experience of capriciousness into a wide variety of new contexts: the stock market, state lotteries, game shows, sporting events, selective service call-ups, traffic lights, movie fads, doctors' fees, clothing fashions. And the potential sphere of the unpredictable and accidental is enormously enlarged: power blackouts, oil spills, computer quirks, nuclear wastes, plane crashes, auto mishaps, chemical poisoning, lung cancer. Human progress, while attempting to bring things "under control" and give life greater predictability and security, has also succeeded in greatly increasing the number of arenas in which to encounter the arbitrary.

This is the ironic ambiguity that is already sensed in the figure of the trickster. Thus his fortunes are unpredictable, and his thefts commonly have ambiguous results. No matter how much structure and order we give our lives, no matter how much meaning and purpose and direction we see or think we see, no matter how successful we believe ourselves to be in making sense out of life or in making progress in some area or other, our lives and our histories still manage to move in mysterious and unforeseen ways. And "the best laid schemes o' mice an' men gang aft a-gley."

So, like our most primitive forebears, we try in various ways to outwit evil forces, encourage good fortune, and obtain guidance by a miscellany of techniques. We cross our fingers, buy dashboard saints, kiss dice, and build apartment houses without a thirteenth floor. We carry trinket charms, wear lucky hats, and cross ourselves before taking a turn at bat. We look for signs and omens, pray for special favors, and diligently consult the daily horoscope. "If I hadn't carried an umbrella today, it would have rained." Or, "If I hadn't been carrying this Testament in the shirt pocket of my fatigues, the bullet would have gotten me." In similar ways, we fancy ourselves to be capable of tricking the weather or the Grim Reaper and otherwise gaining some mysterious control over the stray happenings of our lives.

Even those of us who have lost all remembrance of the ancient trickster and are instead the proud inheritors of vast efforts to bring existence under the orderly procession of scientific knowledge and technological control, are as much of a mystery and problem to ourselves as before. Perhaps we have become *more* of a mystery and problem to ourselves than before. And life seems to insist on being as arbitrary and accidental as ever. There are still the rich and the poor, winners and losers, geniuses and imbeciles, the sane and the insane, beauty queens and ugly ducklings, the gluttonous and the starving, the healthy and the sickly, athletes and paraplegics, those who live a full life and those who die in youth or infancy.

"Who sinned, this man or his parents?" is a question that is probably as old as human consciousness in its effort at comprehending the uneven fortunes of life. And if we do not, perhaps cannot, answer in the simple terms of sin and judgment or karmic consequences or the determinations of the stars, we respond with the images of arbitrariness: "What have we done to deserve this?" "My number came up." "The deck was stacked against me." "Some people are just born lucky." "I'm a born loser." "You win some and you lose some." "Somebody up there likes me." "Somebody up there has it in for me." "I'm having a lucky streak." "I've been down on my luck lately." "That's the breaks."

If we make a special effort to speak more scientifically, we talk of probabilities or percentages. The arbitrariness of a given case is by no means reduced in this fashion, but we are comforted when we express the matter in rational, orderly terms. "The National Safety Council predicts a traffic death toll of 450 over the holiday weekend." Or, "There is a 70 percent chance of rain tomorrow." By developing statistical surveys of the data and a calculus of probabilities, we are able to create the impression of having made sense out of the whole. We have provided a structure of likelihood and unlikelihood. "One out of every three people will die of heart disease." It does not tell us which people, but we feel better already.

Life, as we continue to remark in the most everyday experience, is "just one thing after another," with all its twists and turns, inequities and imponderables, surprises and incongruities. We may abstract slender threads of some pattern and design out of the miscellaneous patches of our existence, but these abstractions still leave the majority of our experiences in a kind of grab-bag pile of scraps and loose ends. Bravely arranged and stitched as the pieces may be, in the resulting patchwork of our lives may yet be seen the silhouetted forms of tricksters and shapeshifters.

Divine Arbitrariness

Life has probably always suggested itself as being in some measure the result of a series of tricks, but this does not necessarily imply a view of life as a "dirty trick" or a "cruel joke" or a "terrible hoax." This may even reflect a profound perception of life as similar to a magician's trick that evokes a sense of awe and wonder rather than betrayal or disillusionment. Things come into being out of an apparent nothing, change shape through some magical metamorphosis, proceed along only partially predictable paths, intermingle in a seemingly infinite network of relationships, and defy any final explanation as to why they are this way rather than that, here rather than there, now rather than then, or anywhere at all.

The trickster symbolizes in a primitive fashion the mystery of being, including the mystery of human being, experienced as an amazing and humorous surprise. While by means of a story an attempt is made to account for things being such and such, and the answers propose some cause or other, still no final *reason* is presented or presentable. Things "just happened" that way.

What, after all, is the "point" or "meaning" to be assigned to even the tiniest wild flower—on the basis of which we might imagine ourselves capable of understanding and perhaps affirming its existence, finding a place for it in the overall scheme of things, and demonstrating the manner in which it contributes to and is caught up in some destiny of the whole—a wild flower that, like the millions of generations that have preceded it, pushes its delicate face up to the sunlight filtering into the forest glade and dares anyone to make sense out of it? Into what cosmic plan does one fit the millennia of dinosaurs who were so long lords of the planet, or the teeming life of the sea? What is the meaning in the meandering path of the mountain stream, or in the sermon being given in the babbling nonsense of the brook? What is the purpose of the millions of galaxies and their billions of stars, or the use of the millions of common flies and their billions of eggs? And what of all the waste space in space— if not as a sign of the sheer thereness or not-thereness of things that stubbornly refuse to conform to our rational patterns and designs or to our egoistic presumption that all things should defer to our moral and intellectual requirements?

The fact that we exist at all to ask questions and propose answers—existing without our self-conscious consent, without even a registry of prior opinion as to time and place and parentage, let alone a choice of individual traits, abilities, and surrounding circumstances—has surely always presented itself as the trick of tricks. The result—as modern societies would express it—of a random impregnation of an ovum by one of hundreds of thousands of possible sperms, we eventually wake up, as it were, to find ourselves existing, male or female, and afforded with this peculiar set of capacities and incapacities. And we must now make our way within a particular mix of individuals and situations, among an infinity of other imaginable individuals and situations, most of which we have not chosen and over which we have little or no control.

In Kurt Vonnegut's *Cat's Cradle*, God has just created Adam, who, upon coming to life and looking around blinking, asks, "What is the *purpose* of all this?" God questions in return, "Everything must have a purpose?" "Certainly," said Adam emphatically. God said, "Then I leave it to you to think of one for all this." And God went away.[5] The issue, however, is not purpose versus purposelessness, but extrinsic versus intrinsic purpose. In the comic vision the meaning of life, like the meaning of art, is primarily within itself, within the spirit and process of living. The purpose of life is fundamentally to live, just as the purpose of the dance is to dance—not to arrive at last at some distant point on the dance floor.

This does not imply the loss of some sublime meaning and purpose without which life becomes dark and aimless and absurd, but it is a gain. It is the highest level of existence, just as the highest level of art is for itself rather than some object beyond itself. If matters were otherwise, life would be lived for a goal outside itself and therefore turned into a perpetual means to some other end, rather than being first and foremost a legitimate end in itself. That is, it would be devalued. And its freedom to be for itself would be forfeited, like reducing art to commercial art or playing football for the money and the glory of Chicago. Life would be given the appearance of having meaning and purpose, but the meaning—however glorious—would always lie elsewhere, and life would be turned into a passageway to this elsewhere. Then if that meaning and purpose were to be lost or placed in doubt, life would become empty indeed, for life would already have been emptied by the presupposition that it can only have meaning and purpose if it serves some other end.

It is true that participants in a game may feel it necessary to justify their particular sport, and all the time, energy, and money expended upon it, by arguing that certain external goals are in fact achieved: teamwork, physical fitness, character development, sportsmanship, group pride, school spirit, sense of achievement, even good citizenship. Yet these are rationalizations for what requires no special reasons or purposes to function and to come into being in the first place. The purpose of a game is to play the game. Playing a game for the sake of the game is the heart of the action, its beginning and end. Only if one stands completely outside the spirit and play of the game does it become in itself meaningless and seemingly absurd, like golf to a golf widow.

Mythologies, of course, attempt to give reasons for things being as they are, and attempt to define the significance and value of this or that aspect of life, and even of life as a whole. For example, "Why do human beings—who are so much more like dogs than lizards—have hands like lizards rather than paws like dogs?" "Because," according to the Yokut Indians, "there was a contest between the dog and the lizard, and the lizard won." The storied explanation makes sense out of the situation. But while a certain cause is assigned and a logic of relationships developed, a fundamental arbitrariness is quite transparent. Whatever the reasons given for some aspect of life having the particular characteristics that it does, one can always ask why it could not have been otherwise, or for some other reason. Sooner or later one comes to the level where no final reasons can be offered. Reasons become either a hat-upon-hat of further questions ("Why did God create the world?" "Because God was lonely and bored") or an admission that no further answers can be given ("God created the world for the hell of it").

The problem is on the order of Mark Twain's playful speculations about the reason oyster shells were to be found five hundred feet above sea level at Smyrna:

I am reduced at last to one slender theory: that the oysters climbed up there of their own accord. But what object could they have had in view?

What did they want to climb a hill for? To climb a hill must necessarily be fatiguing and annoying exercise for an oyster. The most natural conclusion would be that the oysters climbed up there to look at the scenery. Yet when one comes to reflect upon the nature of an oyster, it seems plain that he does not care for scenery. An oyster has no taste for such things. . . . An oyster is of a retiring disposition, and not lively—not even cheerful above the average, and never enterprising. But above all an oyster does not take any interest in scenery. He scorns it. What have I arrived at now? Simply at the point I started from, namely, those oyster shells are there.[6]

Though the trickster is credited with a variety of things being what they are, the elements of *arbitrariness* and *sheer thereness* pervade the vision of life which he represents. Most of the things for which he is "responsible" for having invented or set in motion are not the result of some master plan or carefully calculated purpose or unfolding cosmic destiny. They are the result of chance events, accidents, mistakes, decisions of the moment. Things "just happened" that way. The tales of the trickster personify the ultimate inability to give reasons for things beyond a certain point, reasons that settle once and for all why there is something rather than nothing, or any one particular thing, let alone this incredible variety of things—reasons which would make it finally impossible for someone, even a small child, to ask "But why?" once more.

Religion arises out of a profound sense of the mystery of existence—the mystery of existence as such and the mystery of every existing thing. Yet though an attempt may be made to respond to this mystery by offering interpretations of life which somehow "reveal" this mystery, the mystery is never exhausted or overcome. No amount of philosophical reasoning or scientific investigation or religious inquiry can net it and capture it and add it to the informational zoo of human knowledge. We are not confronted with mystery in the sense of a problem to be solved, a puzzle to be put together, or a detective story that discloses the culprit on the final page. This mystery stands at the beginning and the end of all thought. It represents the limit, the final reaches, of every reason and truth. Insofar as myths offer themselves as the ultimate answer and truth, it is properly so in the sense that they function on the last horizon of human understanding, where all understanding proceeds from and is returned to the *mysterium* out of which it has come.

Such a sense of mystery is, however, not darkness but light, not a burden but a joy, for one is freed from the awesome responsibility of having the last word, the final say, and therefore delivered from the necessity of defending this unquestionable truth against all detractors and from the impulse to play God relative to the universe. One is free to be fully and simply human. In that freedom, nothing is ever completely closed off, finished, wrapped up, sealed. The adventure always remains, the search continues unending, the secret is inexhaustible. One is truly free to laugh before that Mystery of Mysteries which forever eludes and surprises us and which can overwhelm us even in the most obvious, taken-for-granted, and therefore presumably well-known regions of our experience. Here even a mouse, as Walt Whitman put it, "is miracle enough to stagger sextillions of infidels."[7]

Notes

Acknowledgments

1. Charles Chaplin, *My Autobiography* (New York: Simon & Schuster, 1964), p. 399.

Prologue: The Gift of Laughter

1. W.C. Fields, *W. C. Fields by Himself: His Intended Autobiography*, ed. Ronald J. Fields (Englewood Cliffs, N.J.: Prentice-Hall, 1973), p. 235.

2. William Austin Smith, "The Use of the Comic Spirit in Religion," *Atlantic Monthly*, vol. CVIII (August 1911), p. 188.

3. Georg Friedrich Meier, *Thoughts on Jesting* (1794), ed. Joseph Jones (Austin: University of Texas Press, 1947), pp. 55-56.

4. Roland Dixon, *Oceanic Mythology* (Boston: Marshall Jones Co., 1916), p. 15.

5. For the full account of the myth, see Morris E. Opler, *Myths and Tales of the Jicarilla Apache Indians* (New York: American Folklore Society, 1938), pp. 4-8.

6. For a fuller text see Conrad Hyers, ed., *Holy Laughter: Essays on Religion in the Comic Perspective* (New York: Seabury Press, 1969), pp. 252-61.

7. Quoted in Hugo Rahner, *Man at Play* (New York: Herder & Herder, 1965), p. 98.

8. Elton Trueblood, *The Humor of Christ* (New York: Harper & Row, 1964).

9. Bharata, *Natya Shastra*, VI, vv. 61-62.

10. Bartholomaeus Anglicus, *De Proprietatibus Rerum* 5.41.61.

11. Arnold Van Gennep, *Mythes et légendes d'Australia* (Paris, 1906), pp. 84-85.

Chapter 1 A Voice Laughing in the Wilderness

1. Ken Kesey, *One Flew over the Cuckoo's Nest* (New York: Viking Press, 1962), p. 65.

2. Konrad Lorenz, *On Aggression*, trans. Marjorie K. Wilson (New York: Harcourt, Brace Jovanovich, Inc., 1966), pp. 293ff.

3. George Santayana, *Soliloquies in England and Later Soliloquies* (New York: Charles Scribner's Sons, 1922), p. 138.

4. Pat F. Garrett, *An Authentic Life of Billy the Kid* (Santa Fe: New Mexico Printing and Publishing Co., 1882), p. 5.

5. Anthony M. Ludovici, *The Secret of Laughter* (London: Constable & Co., 1932).

6. Sören Kierkegaard, *Concluding Unscientific Postscript*, trans. D.F. Swenson and W. Lowrie (Princeton: Princeton University Press, 1941), p. 413.

7. Al Capp, "The Comedy of Charlie Chaplin," *Atlantic Monthly*, February 1950, pp. 25-29.

8. Gordon W. Allport, *The Individual and His Religion* (New York: Macmillan, 1950), p. 93.

9. Reinhold Niebuhr, *Discerning the Signs of the Times* (London: SCM Press, 1946), pp. 99-100.

10. Harold W. Watts, "The Sense of Regain: A Theory of Comedy," *University of Kansas City Review*, vol. XIII (Autumn 1946), p. 22.

11. Joseph Campbell, *The Hero with a Thousand Faces* (New York: Pantheon, 1949), p. 28.

12. Robert Blake, *101 Elephant Jokes* (New York: Scholastic Book Services, 1964), pp. 8-9. Used by permission.

13. James Thurber, *Lanterns and Lances* (New York: Harper & Bros., 1955), p. 61.

14. Wylie Sypher, ed., *Comedy* (New York: Doubleday, 1956), p. 214.

15. Northrop Frye, *The Anatomy of Criticism* (Princeton: Princeton University Press, 1957), p. 166.

16. Joseph Campbell, *The Masks of God: Primitive Mythology* (New York: Viking Press, 1959), pp. 39-40.

17. Johan Huizinga, *Homo Ludens: A Study of the Play Element in Culture* (Boston: Beacon Press, 1955), p. 119.

Chapter 2 Jester to the Kingdoms of Earth

1. Knud Rasmussen, *The Intellectual Culture of the Iglulik Eskimos* (Copenhagen: Gyldendalski Boghandel, 1929), p. 10.

2. John Doran, *The History of Court Fools* (London: Richard Bentley, 1858), p. 352. For more extensive discussions of the fool see Enid Welsford, *The Fool: His Social and Literary History* (Gloucester, Mass.: Peter Smith, 1966); William Willeford, *The Fool and His Scepter* (Evanston: Northwestern University Press, 1969); Barbara Swain, *Fools and Folly During the Middle Ages and the Renaissance* (New York: Columbia University Press, 1932).

3. Erica Tietze-Conrat, *Dwarfs and Jesters in Art* (New York: Phaidon, 1957), p. 70.

4. Wylie Sypher, ed., *Comedy* (New York: Doubleday, 1956), p. 221.

5. Max Gluckman, *Rituals of Rebellion in South-East Africa* (Manchester: Manchester University Press, 1954), p. 27. Cf. Max Gluckman, *Customs and Conflicts in Africa* (Glencoe, Ill.: Free Press, 1955).

6. Tietze-Conrat, *Dwarfs and Jesters in Art*, p. 66.

7. Gladys Reichard, *Navaho Religion: A Study of Symbolism*, vol. 2 (New York: Pantheon, 1950), pp. 491-92.

8. Alfred Metraux, "Voodoo in Haiti," in *Anthropology of Folk Religion*, ed. Charles Leslie (New York: Random House, 1960), pp. 439-40.

9. A.P. Rossiter, *English Drama from Early Times to the Elizabethans* (New York: Barnes & Noble, 1950), pp. 56-60.

10. G. P. Fedotov, *The Russian Religious Mind*, vol. II: *The Middle Ages* (Cambridge, Mass.: Harvard University Press, 1966), pp. 316-43. See also John Sayward, *Perfect Fools: Folly for Christ's Sake in Catholic and Orthodox Spirituality* (New York: Oxford University Press, 1980).

11. C.S. Lewis, *The Screwtape Letters* (New York: Macmillan, 1944), p. 7.

12. Reinhold Niebuhr, *Discerning the Signs of the Times* (London: SCM Press, 1946), p. 99.

13. Harold W. Watts, "The Sense of Regain: A Theory of Comedy," *University of Kansas City Review*, vol. XIII (Autumn 1946), p. 20.

14. William Austin Smith, "The Use of the Comic Spirit in Religion," *Atlantic Monthly*, August 1911, p. 188.

15. Paul Tillich, *Dynamics of Faith* (New York: Harper & Bros., 1957).

16. *The Praise of Folly*, trans. Hoyt H. Hudson (Princeton: Princeton University Press, 1941), sec. 28, p. 78.

17. Quoted in Swain, *Fools and Folly*, p. 219, n. 42.

18. Quoted in ibid., p. 215, n. 19.

19. *Portrait of Karl Barth*, trans. Robert McAfee Brown and George Casalis, (New York: Doubleday, 1963), p. 3.

20. Gerardus van Der Leeuw, *Religion in Essence and Manifestation*, trans. J.E. Turner (New York: Harper & Row, 1963), 2:680.

Chapter 3 Putting Humpty-Dumpty Together Again

1. Robert Payne, *The Great God Pan* (New York: Hermitage House, 1952), pp. 21-22.

2. N. Ross Crumrine, "Capakoba, the Mayo Easter Ceremonial Impersonator: Explanations of Ritual Clowning," *Journal for the Scientific Study of Religion*, vol. VIII, no. 1 (Spring 1969), pp. 1-22.

3. Payne, *The Great God Pan*, p. 20.

4. Albert Reagan, "Notes on Jemez Ethnography," *American Anthropologist*, n.s. xxix (1927), pp. 723-24.

5. Elsie Clews Parsons, *Pueblo Indian Religion* (Chicago: University of Chicago Press, 1939), vol. I, pp. 95, 246.

6. For an extensive discussion of the Pueblo clowns see Frank Bock, A *Descriptive Study of the Dramatic Function and Significance of the Clown During Hopi Indian Public Ceremony* (Ph.D. diss., University of Southern California, 1971).

7. Reprinted from *Leaves of Grass* by Walt Whitman, ed. Harold W. Blodgett and Sculley Bradley. Copyright © 1965 by New York University. Reprinted by permission of New York University Press.

8. Claude Levi-Strauss, *Structural Anthropology*, vol. 1 (New York: Basic Books, 1963), pp. 202-27.

9. Payne, *The Great God Pan*, p. 12.

10. Charles Chaplin, *My Autobiography* (New York: Simon & Schuster, 1964), p. 144.

11. In Conrad Hyers, ed., *Holy Laughter: Essays on Religion in the Comic Perspective* (New York: Seabury Press, 1969), p. 77.

12. John Gardner, *The Sunlight Dialogues* (New York: Knopf, 1972).

13. Frank H. Cushing, "Outline of Zuni Creation Myths," *13th Annual Report of the Bureau of American Ethnology* (Washington: U.S. Government Printing Office, 1896), p. 402.

14. Elsie Clews Parson and Ralph L. Beals, "The Sacred Clowns of the Pueblo and Mayo-Yaqui Indians," *American Anthropologist*, vol. 36 (October-December 1934), p. 493.

15. Nathan Scott, Jr., *The Broken Center* (New Haven: Yale University Press, 1966), p. 90.

Chapter 4 A Fool's Liturgy

1. Carmen B. De Gasztold, *Prayers from the Ark*, trans. Rumer Godden (New York: Viking Press, 1962), p. 53.

2. Harvey Cox, *The Feast of Fools: A Theological Essay on Festivity and Fantasy* (Cambridge: Harvard University Press, 1969), pp. 22-24.

3. Adrien Wettach, *Life's a Lark* (New York: Benjamin Blom, 1969), pp. 17, 52.

4. *Mark Twain's "Which Was the Dream?"* ed. John S. Tuckey (Berkeley: University of California Press, 1966), p. 57.

5. Nikos Kazantzakis, *Zorba the Greek*, trans. Carl Wedman (New York: Simon & Schuster, 1952), p. 151.

6. William Wordsworth, "Ode: Intimations of Immortality from Recollections of Early Childhood," *Wordsworth's Poetical Works*, ed. E. de Selincourt and Helen Darbishire (London: Oxford University Press, 1947), vol. IV, p. 281. Used by permission.

7. Sören Kierkegaard, *Concluding Unscientific Postscript*, trans. D.F. Swenson and W. Lowrie (Princeton: Princeton University Press, 1941), p. 553.

8. George Santayana, *Soliloquies in England and Later Soliloquies* (New York: Charles Scribner's, 1922), pp. 141-42.

9. Elder Olson, *The Theory of Comedy* (Bloomington: Indiana University Press, 1968), p. 36.

10. For an extended interpretation of comic elements in Zen Buddhism see my *Zen and the Comic Spirit* (London: Rider & Co., 1973; Philadelphia: Westminster Press, 1974).

11. John C.H. Wu, *The Golden Age of Zen* (Taipei: National War College, 1967), p. 203.

12. Reprinted from *Leaves of Grass* by Walt Whitman, ed. Harold W. Blodgett and Sculley Bradley. Copyright © 1965 by New York University. Reprinted by permission of New York University Press.

13. Friedrich Nietzsche, *Thus Spake Zarathustra*, trans. Thomas Common (New York: Random House, n.d.), p. 25.

Chapter 5 Will the Real Adam and Eve Please Stand Up?

1. George Steiner, *The Death of Tragedy* (New York: Alfred A. Knopf, 1963), p. 247.

2. Nathan Scott, Jr., *The Broken Center* (New Haven: Yale University Press, 1966), pp. 101, 103.

3. Cf. Barbara Swain, *Fools and Folly During the Middle Ages and the Renaissance* (New York: Columbia University Press, 1932).

4. Donald Keene, ed., *Essays in Idleness: The Tsurezuregusa of Kenko,* trans. Donald Keene (New York: Columbia University Press, 1967), p. 7.

5. Quoted in Walter Kerr, *Tragedy and Comedy* (New York: Simon & Schuster, 1967), p. 152.

6. John Dominic Crossan, *Raid on the Articulate: Comic Eschatology in Jesus and Borges* (New York: Harper & Row, 1976), p. 30.

7. William F. Lynch, *Christ and Apollo: The Dimensions of the Literary Imagination* (New York: Sheed & Ward, 1960), p. 109.

8. Friedrich Nietzsche, *Beyond Good and Evil: Prelude to a Philosophy of the Future* (New York: Random House, 1966), p. 41.

9. *The Gospel of Sri Ramakrishna,* abridged edition, ed. Swami Nikhilananda (New York: Ramakrishna-Vivekananda Center, 1942), p. 23.

Chapter 6 Between Dreams and Dust

1. Munro Leaf, *The Story of Ferdinand* (New York: Viking Press, 1936).

2. Cf. Joseph Campbell, *The Hero with a Thousand Faces,* rev. ed. (Princeton: Princeton University Press, 1968).

3. Ibid.

4. Joseph Meeker, *The Comedy of Survival* (New York: Charles Scribner's Sons, 1972), p. 26.

5. See Martin Buber, *The Tales of Rabbi Nachman* (Bloomington, Ind.: Indiana University Press, 1962), pp. 71ff.

6. Herbert Read, *Art Now: An Introduction to the Theory of Modern Painting* (New York: Pitman, 1960), p. 10.

7. Mircea Eliade, *The Sacred and the Profane* (New York: Harper & Row, 1961), pp. 10-11.

8. Conrad Hyers, *Zen and the Comic Spirit* (London: Rider & Co., 1973; Philadelphia: Westminster Press, 1974), p. 84.

9. Karl von Frisch, *A Biologist Remembers,* trans. Lisbeth Gombrich (Elmsford, N.Y.: Pergamon Press, 1967), p. 12.

10. William James, *The Varieties of Religious Experience* (New York: Longman's & Green, 1902).

11. Abraham H. Maslow, *Toward a Psychology of Being,* 2d ed. (New York: D. van Nostrand Co., 1968), p. 102.

12. Ibid., p. 92.

13. Ibid., p. 80.

14. *Psychology Today,* August 1970, p. 16.

15. Martin Grotjahn, *Beyond Laughter: A Psychoanalytical Approach to Humor* (New York: McGraw-Hill, 1966), pp. 205ff.

16. Meeker, *The Comedy of Survival*, p. 25.

17. *The Christian Century*, May 22, 1974, p. 570.

18. T. S. Eliot, "Little Gidding," *Collected Poems 1909-1962* (New York: Harcourt, Brace Jovanovich, 1963), pp. 208-9. Used by permission.

Chapter 7 Tragic Castles and Comic Cottages

1. The first English version of this tale appeared in Antwerp in 1492. See Enid Welsford, *The Fool: His Social and Literary History*. (Gloucester, Mass.: Peter Smith, 1966), pp. 35-37, n. 331.

2. Cf. Walter Kerr, *Tragedy and Comedy* (New York: Simon & Schuster, 1967), p. 125.

3. *Hegel: On Tragedy*, ed. Anne and Henry Paolucci (New York: Harper & Row, 1962), pp. 52-53.

4. Luigi Pirandello, "The Art of Humor," *Massachusetts Review* (March 1952), p. 518.

5. Ibid., p. 519.

6. Welsford, *The Fool*, pp. 324-26.

7. Alan W. Watts, *The Way of Zen* (New York: Random House, 1957), p. 147.

8. Harold G. Henderson, *An Introduction to Haiku* (New York: Doubleday, 1958), p. 183.

Chapter 8 A Divine Comedy

1. S. Radhakrishnan, *Eastern Religions and Western Thought* (New York: Oxford University Press, 1939).

2. Cf. Conrad Hyers, *Zen and the Comic Spirit* (London: Rider & Co., 1973; Philadelphia: Westminster Press, 1974), chaps. 3-5.

3. Friedrich Nietzsche, *The Antichrist*, trans. R.J. Hollingdale (New York: Penguin Books, 1968), p. 128.

4. Paul Ricoeur, "The Parables," *Criterion*, (Spring 1974), p. 19. See also Dan O. Via, Jr., *Kerygma and Comedy in the New Testament: A Structuralist Approach to Hermeneutic* (Philadelphia: Fortress Press, 1975), for an application of comic structure to an interpretation of the parables.

5. Samuel Miller, "The Clown in Contemporary Art," *Holy Laughter: Essays on Religion in the Comic Perspective*, ed. Conrad Hyers (New York: Seabury Press, 1969), p. 96.

6. Hart Crane, "Chaplinesque," *The Complete Poems and Selected Letters and Prose of Hart Crane*, ed. Brom Weber (New York: Liveright Publishing Corp., 1966), p. 11. Used by permission.

Chapter 9 A Happy Ending of Sorts

1. e. e. cummings, "i thank You God" from the *Complete Poems 1913-1962* by E.E. Cummings (New York: Harcourt Brace Jovanovich, 1972), p. 663. Copyright 1947 by E.E. Cummings; renewed 1975 by Nancy T. Andrews. Reprinted by permission of Harcourt Brace Jovanovich, Inc.

2. F.M. Cornford, *The Origin of Attic Comedy* (London: Arnold, 1914).

3. Northrup Frye, *The Anatomy of Criticism* (Princeton: Princeton University Press, 1957), pp. 163-86.

4. Susanne K. Langer, *Feeling and Form* (New York: Charles Scribner's Sons, 1953), p. 331.

5. Wylie Sypher, ed., *Comedy* (New York: Doubleday, 1956), p. 220.

6. Dan O. Via, Jr., *The Parables: Their Literary and Existential Dimension* (Philadelphia: Fortress Press, 1967), pp. 110, 145. Cf. Dan O. Via, Jr., *Kerygma and Comedy in the New Testament: A Structuralist Approach to Hermeneutic* (Philadelphia: Fortress Press, 1975).

7. Via, *Parables*, p. 104.

8. John Dominic Crossan, *Raid on the Articulate: Comic Eschatology in Jesus and Borges* (New York: Harper & Row, 1976), p. 22.

9. *Hegel: On Tragedy*, ed. Anne and Henry Paolucci (New York: Harper & Row, 1962), pp. 48-49, 68-69. Cf. Walter Kerr, *Tragedy and Comedy*, (New York: Simon & Schuster, 1967), pp. 37.

10. Kerr, *Tragedy and Comedy*, p. 104.

11. Cedric H. Whitman, *Aristophanes and the Comic Hero* (Cambridge: Harvard University Press, 1964), p. 57.

12. James Sully, *An Essay on Laughter* (London: Longmans, 1902), p. 384.

13. See Ruth R. Wisse, *The Schlemiel as Modern Hero* (Chicago: University of Chicago Press, 1971), p. 12.

14. Emnett Kelly, *Clown* (New York: Prentice-Hall, 1954), p. 49.

15. Harold W. Watts, "The Sense of Regain: A Theory of Comedy," *University of Kansas City Review*, vol. XIII (Autumn 1946), p. 23.

16. Crossan, *Raid on the Articulate*, p. 32.

17. Quoted in *Eight Great Comedies*, ed. Sylvan Barnet et al. (New York: New American Library, 1958), p. 452.

18. Cf. Eugene Ionesco, *Notes and Counternotes: Writings on the Theater*, trans. Donald Watson (New York: Grove Press, 1964), p. 163.

19. Christopher Fry, "Comedy," in *Comedy: Meaning and Form*, ed. Robert W. Corrigan (San Francisco: Chandler Publishing Co., 1965), p. 15.

Chapter 10 The Game and the Adventure

1. Paul Radin, *The Trickster: A Study in American Indian Mythology* (London: Routledge & Kegan Paul, 1956), p. 164. Mac L. Ricketts, "The North American Indian Trickster," *History of Religions*, vol. 5, no. 2 (University of Chicago, 1966), p. 332.

2. Mark Twain, *Roughing It* (Berkeley: University of California Press, 1972), p. 245.

3. Mircea Eliade, *The Sacred and the Profane* (New York: Harper & Row, 1961).

4. Nikos Kazantzakis, *Zorba the Greek*, trans. Carl Wedman (New York: Simon & Schuster, 1952), p. 152.

5. Kurt Vonnegut, Jr., *Cat's Cradle* (New York: Delacorte Press, 1963), pp. 214-15.

6. Mark Twain, *The Innocents Abroad* (New York: Harper & Bros., 1911), 2:133-34.

7. Reprinted from *Leaves of Grass* by Walt Whitman, ed. Harold W. Blodgett and Sculley Bradley. Copyright © 1965 by New York University. Reprinted by permission of New York University Press.

Aichele, George, Jr. *Theology As Comedy: Critical and Theoretical Implications.* Washington, D.C.: University Press of America, 1980.

Babcock, Barbara A., ed. *The Reversible World: Ritual Inversion in Art and Society.* Ithaca: Cornell University Press, 1978.

Corrigen, Robert W., ed. *Comedy: Meaning and Form.* San Francisco: Chandler Press, 1965.

Cox, Harvey. *The Feast of Fools: A Theological Essay on Festivity and Fantasy.* Cambridge: Harvard University Press, 1969.

Crossan, John Dominic. *Raid on the Articulate: Comic Eschatology in Jesus and Borges.* New York: Harper & Row, 1976.

Erasmus, Desiderius. *Praise of Folly.* Translated by John Wilson. Ann Arbor: University of Michigan Press, 1958.

Huizinga, Johan. *Homo Ludens: A Study of the Play Element in Culture.* Boston: Beacon Press, 1950.

Hyers, Conrad, ed. *Holy Laughter: Essays on Religion in the Comic Perspective.* New York: Seabury Press, 1969.

———. *Zen and the Comic Spirit.* London: Rider & Co., 1973; Philadelphia: Westminster Press, 1974.

Lynch, William F. *Christ and Apollo: Dimensions of the Literary Imagination.* New York: Sheed & Ward, 1969.

McLelland, Joseph C. *The Clown and the Crocodile.* Atlanta: John Knox Press, 1970.

Meeker, Joseph. *The Comedy of Survival.* New York: Charles Scribner's Sons, 1972.

Miller, David L. *Gods and Games: Toward a Theology of Play.* New York: Harper & Row, 1974.

Pelton, Robert D. *The Trickster in West Africa: Sacred Irony and Mythic Delight.* Berkeley: University of California Press, 1980.

Radin, Paul. *The Trickster: A Study in American Indian Mythology.* New York: Schocken Books, 1972.

Rahner, Hugo. *Man at Play.* New York: Herder & Herder, 1965.

Sayward, John. *Perfect Fools: Folly for Christ's Sake in Catholic and Orthodox Spirituality.* New York: Oxford University Press, 1980.

Swabey, Marie C. *Comic Laughter: A Philosophical Essay.* New Haven: Yale University Press, 1961.

Towsen, John H. *Clowns: A Panoramic History.* New York: Hawthorn Books, 1976.

Trueblood, Elton. *The Humor of Christ.* New York: Harper & Row, 1964.

Via, Dan O., Jr. *Kerygma and Comedy in the New Testament.* Philadelphia: Fortress Press, 1975.

Vos, Nelvin. *The Drama of Comedy: Victim and Victor.* Atlanta: John Knox Press, 1966.

Welsford, Enid. *The Fool: His Social and Literary History.* Gloucester, Mass.: Peter Smith, 1966.

Willeford, William. *The Fool and His Scepter: A Study in Clowns and Jesters and Their Audience.* Evanston: Northwestern University Press, 1969.